In Praise of *The Leader*

D1399414

"An extraordinary collection of truly inspiring insights into leadership success; an instant classic."

Lauren M. Doliva, PhD, Heidrick & Struggles

"This is truly an important book for our times. Given decades of erosion in the principles and practices of corporate and public leadership, Bruna's book reminds us, in fact inspires us, about the salient characteristics of trusted leaders and the forces that drive us to follow and respect them. This book is a must-read for everyone. We all have the opportunity to lead each day and Bruna shows us our potential to do so."

Michael H. Mitchell, Founder, GreenLight Management Inc.

"I often read leadership books and wonder whether I would want to lead in such a way, whether I would be capable of such leadership, or whether I would follow such a leader. In this book, Bruna Martinuzzi has woven the essential meaning of the word 'Mensch' into a new vision for leaders. I am confident that such leaders would be 'worth following.'"

David R. Caruso, PhD, EI Skills Group
Co-author, *The Emotionally Intelligent Manager*
Co-author, *MEIS* and *MSCEIT*

"Bruna Martinuzzi has distilled the essence of what it takes to influence and motivate others, not by the exercise of authority, but through the example of ethical and admirable character. She doesn't just tell us how—she helps us understand."

Mark D. Lange, MBA, Writer, *Christian Science Monitor*
Former PeopleSoft and SAP Executive

"A deeply profound book for coaches, mentors, as well as senior executives and emergent leaders. The truth is, it's a must-read for anyone in society who has opportunity to influence others."

Larry M. Bienati, PhD, Consultants to Management
Author, *When Eagles Fly in Formation*

The Leader as a Mensch

Become the Kind of Person
Others Want to Follow

Bruna Martinuzzi

Foreword by
Michael A. Freeman, MD, CEO

Six Seconds Emotional Intelligence Press
San Francisco, CA

The Leader as a Mensch
Become the Kind of Person Others Want to Follow

First printed January 2009.

The paper used in this book meets the minimum requirements of the American National Standard for Information Services—Permanence of Paper for Printed Library Materials, ANSI Z39.48-1984.

Library of Congress Control Number: 2008943006

Book design and interior photos by David B. Page.
www.beeherd.biz

ISBN 9780979734304
Printed and bound in the United States.

Six Seconds Emotional Intelligence Press
San Francisco, California

Dedication

To Saul, of course.
You show me every day
what it is to be a Mensch.

"Ever seen a leaf—a leaf from a tree?"
"Yes."
*"I saw one recently—a yellow one, a little green, wilted at
the edges. Blown by the wind. When I was a little boy,
I used to shut my eyes in winter and imagine a green leaf,
with veins on it, and the sun shining..."*
"What's this—an allegory?"
*"No; why? Not an allegory—a leaf, just a leaf.
A leaf is good. Everything's good."*

-Fyodor Dostoevsky-
The Possessed Dialogue between Kirolov and Stavrogin

Contents

Foreword

In this crisp, concise book about how to become the kind of leader that others want to follow, Bruna Martinuzzi recognizes that before you can lead any group, any team, or any organization, you must first lead yourself. You must learn to be the CEO of your own life, to have a purpose that is larger than your own ambition, and to develop the humility, integrity, and mission-driven determination that instills hope and confidence in others. The strength, wisdom and self-mastery of Mensch-like leadership are not effected for personal benefit. Instead, they are the building blocks used to construct a better external reality. Mensch-like leadership is the foundation of a humanitarian effort to contribute and to be of service to others.

Mensch leadership is not about 'me'. It is about 'us'. *The Leader as a Mensch* illustrates the qualities of integrity and honor, decency and reliability, empathy and appreciation, selflessness and service that allow men and women at any level in any organization to influence and motivate others not by the exercise of authority, but by the example of being an upstanding individual with an admirable character. Mensch leaders are calm and credible. They make us feel safe, hopeful, appreciated, and good about ourselves. They appeal to our better angels and show us how to align our personal mission with a broader community purpose.

Bruna Martinuzzi speaks six languages in addition to the language of the heart. She glides across the wisdom of leadership the way a champion figure skater glides across the ice. In *The Leader as a Mensch,* Ms. Martinuzzi overcomes the hazard of being lost in translation by communicating a tangible, palpable, and practical understanding of leadership from the inside out.

Bruna's father is Italian, her mother is Greek, she was raised in

Egypt, she spoke French at home, she was taught in German, and she writes in English. In this brief and accessible book, she reaches across her matrix of experience and meaning to unpack the guidelines for emotionally intelligent leadership from within the Yiddish concept of being a Mensch. As Bruna explains, a Mensch is a powerful leader who inspires with the integrity and confidence and force of character that motivates others to follow—not through persuasion or intimidation, but by the example of consistent, courageous, compassionate confidence. Her message elaborates on the message of Rabbi Hillel: "If I am not for myself, who will be for me? If I am only for myself, who am I? If not now, when?"

The approach to leadership described in this book is nothing new. In fact, it is prehistoric. Twenty thousand generations ago our human ancestors pushed forward from the African Rift Valley to begin our global—now galactic—Diaspora. Eons before the advent of MBA programs and leadership training workshops, leaders inspired their clans, bands, and tribes to take the risk of moving into an unknown world in which opportunity outweighed risk and where the community could flourish even if the leader expired along the way.

Over time, a fundamental difference developed between those who left and those who stayed behind, a difference encoded in the brain at the level of dopamine receptors and limbic regulation. In this prehistoric leadership environment, some tribes stayed behind to establish comfortable lives with known and routinized business models in familiar ancestral environments. They evolved the patterns of culture that dominated old Africa, old Mesopotamia, and old Europe. Later in history, their progeny would sink into the rust belt obsolescence of old Agriculture, old Industry, old Religion and old Empire—only to implode under the tsunami of disruptive innovations that washed over their establishments from those who moved on. Perhaps the leaders and followers who stayed behind were motivated by a lust for power, a fear of the unknown, the reassurance of tradition and the security of a familiar way of life. They did not ask "if not now, when?" They clung to a paradigm they perceived to be eternal; a culture that they believed has always been and will always be.

Those who moved on were different. They knew that they were crowded out of the supply chain by a defensive elite establishment that guarded its resources jealously. The nomads could also contrast the world as it is with the world as it could be. They perceived their external reality as a reservoir of opportunity not for themselves, but for their people. Rather than stay and fight for a bigger share of a smaller pie, they found the courage to inspire their loved ones to adapt, to experiment, to change, to explore, and to improve. This ability to lead without the formal investment of power was facilitated by the personal qualities of the leader that Bruna Martinuzzi discusses in her book: humility, authenticity, empathy, accountability, optimism, mastery, mood management, emotional intelligence, generosity, and appreciation. Their power to lead flowed from their broadly under-stood leadership goal, namely service to the community rather than aggrandizement of the self.

In her classic 1934 study, *Patterns of Culture*, anthropologist Ruth Benedict described this Mensch-like leadership quality in the pre-historic culture of the Zuni tribe of Native Americans. She explains:

"The ideal Zuni is a person of dignity who has never tried to lead and has never called forth comment from his neighbors. A good man has a pleasing address, a yielding disposition, and a generous heart. He should set people at their ease, and he should cooperate easily with others, never betraying a suspicion of arrogance or a strong emotion. He avoids office. He may have it thrust upon him, but he does not seek it."[1]

Mensch-like leaders populate the more recent history of our people. Some of them have guided us through political upheavals, including George Washington, Abraham Lincoln, Winston Churchill, Mahatma Gandhi and Barak Obama. Some of them have given us the courage to navigate mission-critical social transformations, such as Martin Luther King, Oprah Winfrey, Marian Wright Edelman, Rachel Carson, Helen Keller and Susan B. Anthony. We have been inspired by Mensch-like spiritual leaders such as the Dali Lama, Mother Theresa, and Martin Luther King to conduct our own lives from the inner decency and power that derives from a fundamental awareness of the eternal, respect for the interconnectedness of all life, and a direct disintermediated relationship with the divine.

Mensch leadership is also a powerful force for empowerment, equality, human rights, global community building and prosperity in the 21st century economy. For example, David Packard, the co-founder of Hewlett-Packard, embodied the low-key egalitarian Mensch leadership qualities that produced his company's highly-regarded culture of sustained innovation and its steady flow of civilization-changing breakthrough products and services. Mensch leadership qualities are also embodied in the Google leadership team; a team which by any standard has produced astonishing results. In April 2004, the BBC News described Google founders Larry Page and Sergey Brin in terms that seem to flow from the pages of Bruna Martinuzzi's book.[2]

The founders of the Google internet search engine—Larry Page and Sergey Brin—are the type of young men most parents would dream of their daughters bringing home. Most mums and dads would also be drawn to the facts that both men are very clean cut in appearance, undeniably hard working and intelligent, and seem, well, just "nice". They are your text book, well presented, quietly well behaved "boys next door" from a smart middle class American suburb. Only a lot richer.

Yet far from living an extravagant lifestyle, complete with yachts and private jets like fellow software leader Oracle boss Larry Ellison, Mr. Page, 31, and Mr. Brin, 30, are both reported to continue to live modest, unassuming lifestyles. They don't even have sports cars, and instead are said to each drive a Toyota Prius, a plain-looking but rather environmentally friendly saloon that is half electric-powered, and growing in popularity among green-minded Americans. Mr. Brin's father even claimed recently that his son still rents a modest two bedroom apartment.

There is something very 1960s California about what Mr. Page and Mr. Brin say is their philosophy. As Mr. Page recently explained: "We have a mantra: 'Don't be evil', which is to do the best things we know how for our users, for our customers, for everyone. So I think if we were known for that, it would be a wonderful thing."

Readers who prefer to not waste their time will find this book to be a very efficiently written and practical how to guide filled with tools and additional resources. Each chapter includes inspirational vignettes and concrete pointers including practices, exercises and suggestions for developing the core competencies of Mensch-like leadership: humility, authenticity, empathy, accountability, optimism, mastery, mood management, emotional intelligence, generosity, and appreciation. As a result, *The Leader as a Mensch* has something to offer for a wide audience including emergent leaders, senior leaders, and individual contributors.

Bruna Martinuzzi recognizes that we all get distracted and derailed from our noble intentions by competition, organizational politics, economic changes, and the never-ending flow of deadline-driven tasks. *The Leader as a Mensch* gives us the opportunity to stop and think for a moment, to find one competency to practice at a time, and to evolve the way that we show up, both as a leader and as a person.

The Leader as a Mensch was written to be a book for everyone, not just senior and emergent leaders but also coaches, mentors, and anyone in society who has an opportunity to influence others. It serves as an emotional fitness primer that is offered to us by a coach who recognizes that some people have a natural gift for leadership while for others it is a craft that can be learned. This book illustrates the ways in which all of us, at any level can improve our leadership impact through proper intention coupled with study, contemplation, emulation, practice, developing emotional intelligence and learning from mistakes.

Bruna Martinuzzi appreciates the fact that we cannot all be leaders, so this book is written for followers, too. She reminds us that even as followers, we are also all leaders in our own sphere. As followers we can support our peers and lead horizontally among members of our peer group, by sharing skills and knowledge and by standing out as a good team player. Within our groups of whatever kind, we can position ourselves as someone who is recognized for taking the high road, avoiding gossip, supporting others and empowering others to succeed. As followers, we can support the good leaders who bless us with their devotion to the benefit of our community. Good leaders need feedback and support. It takes far less effort for a community to support and sustain a good and Mensch-like leader than to displace a toxic one. Effective followers are a critically important for sustainable good leadership.

Civilization has arrived at a tipping point. We face perilous choices with vast implications for future generations. We confront such 21st century imperatives as the need to demilitarize the world, to rescue the environment, to protect other life forms, to eradicate poverty, to expand human rights, to overcome disease, and to extend the benefits of peace, freedom, security and happiness. Failure to accomplish this mission implies large scale suffering and perhaps catastrophic consequences. Success will require inspirational and effective leadership. The last twenty thousand generations of human leadership have brought us the knowledge and tools we need to move this agenda forward. Much of this knowledge and many of these tools are offered to us, with care and compassion, in Bruna Martinuzzi's book, *The Leader as a Mensch*.

Michael A. Freeman, M.D.

Dr. Freeman is a CEO and performance enhancement coach who primarily works with bipolar spectrum leaders and high achievers in business and the arts. Dr. Freeman serves as an Associate Clinical Professor of Psychiatry at the UCSF School of Medicine. For further information contact Michael.Freeman@marincounty.net.

References:

1. Ruth Benedict, *Patterns of Culture*. (Boston: Houghton Mifflin Company, 1934), 99.
2. Will Smale, "Profile: The Google Founders," BBC News On-Line Front Page, International Version, 20 April, 2004. http://news.bbc.co.uk/1/hi/business/3666241.stm.

Acknowledgments

I am grateful to Joshua Freedman, my publisher, for encouraging me to write this book. I still see his face when he said: "It's time." I would like to thank the entire Six Seconds team for their noble goal to make a positive difference, from here to the remotest regions of the world. I am also indebted to all the leaders who showed me how a Mensch behaves in times of extreme challenges. I am grateful to Ron Crossland (surely "Exhibit A" in Menschhood), for his readiness to help and for modeling appreciative intelligence. I am also grateful to my copyeditor, Mady Gorrell, for editing the manuscript and for her infectious enthusiasm of the material, as well as to Debbie Rand for generously going out of her way to help proofread the manuscript. Special accolades go to David B. Page for his dedication to design and photo excellence; and to the book's entire production team—collectively and individually, they show success is achieved in inches, not miles. I would like to honor too, the many Mensches I have had the fortune to encounter in my life: Durand Gumuchian, who said to me when I was 13, "You will write like Francoise Sagan"; Susanne Cosmai, Libera Ravizzoni, Mohsen Mohamed Hassan, Mohamed and Hussam, icons of Menschhood; Monique Bishara, the quintessential example of the Mensch as a Friend; Marsha Royer, Mark Ahrens-Townsend and James H. Rhodes, exemplary leaders; Martin Taylor, Harvey S. Delaney, and Dr. Alistair MacKay (you are a tribute to your professions); and lastly, my late mother. If I had half of her ability to be a Mensch, I would have reason to be proud.

Introduction

As a child, I heard the word *Mensch* mentioned frequently by my parents. The very first instance is etched in my mind. It was in the early 1950s in Cairo, Egypt. Our neighbor and good friend, Sammy, was visiting us as he usually did every evening. On that evening, however, there was something different about his behavior. He was quieter than usual and when he left to go downstairs to his apartment, he gave each one of us a warm hug, which seemed out of the ordinary. It was my mother who commented that there was something not quite right with Sammy and that she was concerned. The next morning, she woke up and announced that we should check to make sure that Sammy was okay. I accompanied my parents to Sammy's apartment and we were surprised to find the door slightly ajar. We walked in and everything seemed in place. All of his clothes were hanging in the armoire and his briefcase was by the door where he always kept it. But, somehow, we knew he had left for good. We discovered several small pieces of paper that, to a stranger, might have seemed like scraps with random notes. But each one had one of our nicknames at the bottom, or on the side randomly scribbled, just enough for my parents to put two and two together. It was understood that he had fled the country. This was not uncommon for many Jews of that era who, fearing repercussions from local authorities, felt compelled to leave without attracting attention to themselves or the friends who stayed behind. It was the early 1950s, a time when a wave of nationalist xenophobia swept through Cairo. Sammy knew that after he left my parents might be questioned about his departure and that their ignorance of his plans was for their own protection. Still, he wanted to say goodbye, and he did so by leaving the door slightly ajar for us and leaving each one of us a gift, subtly marked. My "note" was on the leather bound dictionary with his gold engraved initials that he had frequently allowed me to look at, while always reminding me to be careful as it was a gift from his father. For my mother, it was the old carved bowl that she used to fill with some of the delicacies he liked. And for my father, it was his Meerschaum pipe. By wanting to protect us, Sammy was noble up to his very last gesture with us. That morning, my father said: "He is a Mensch."

Mensch is a German word meaning human being or person, It has no gender. In Yiddish, it is a popular word with deep connotations. It has been variously translated as a man (or woman) of integrity and honor, an upstanding individual, a decent person with admirable characteristics. It describes an individual who is higher on the evolutionary scale, a person in whose presence we feel safe; a person who makes us we feel good about ourselves. It is someone we want to work for, someone we want as our spouse or business partner– it is someone that we would welcome as a friend. Among the admirable characteristics of a Mensch are humility, authenticity, integrity, fairness, accountability, dependability, conscientiousness, empathy, composure, optimism, generosity, and appreciation—to name a few. There are no organizational assessments for Menschhood. You know when you are in the presence of a Mensch. They have a calm presence and they exude credibility. They earn respect without demanding it. They will often lead from the side, just by the sheer force of their example, whether in the boardroom, classroom or living room. These are individuals with high emotional intelligence. To be called a Mensch, is the greatest compliment one can give you.

This book is an exploration of what it takes to be a Mensch. It is organized around the metaphor of a tree. The tree is our botanical analogue: The *roots* are the anchor; the trunk comprises the main body and the branches and leaves are the extensions. As a Mensch, the roots represent our foundation, that which anchors and nurtures us and gives us our resilience. It's our stability—the most crucial part. Just as a tree cannot survive without its roots, so a leader cannot exist as a leader without these three foundational qualities—humility, authenticity, and empathy. While the roots are underground, the *trunk* is the visible part—the outward manifestation of who we are. It is the body of our leadership ethos in action which others see clearly. It comprises our accountability, our optimism, and our comportment as a leader. And the *branches* are further manifestations of how we stretch ourselves to reach and inspire others as leaders—they represent our moods, our generosity, and our appreciation of others. Our power to influence and inspire those who surround us lives in our branches.

This book is not just for the high-profile executives we hear or read about in the media. It is for the everyday leader. Who are everyday leaders? They are the managers, supervisors or team leaders, the senior leaders with years of experience or the emergent leaders poised for career advancement. They are the community organizers, the people who run our religious establishments and government departments. They are our teachers in charge of young minds; our educators who nurture the next generation. They are the independent business people, the professionals, and the non-profit volunteers. They are the executive assistants, the librarians, and the shopkeepers. In short, they are each one of us. We can all choose to be leaders in our sphere, large or small.

As I write this, we are in the midst of one of the most difficult business debacles and leadership crises in decades. People are concerned and anxious about their economic well-being. Years ago, I read a line in a book which said, "When in doubt, act like the Chairman would." Sadly, this phrase would now elicit derision when we ponder the moral depravity of leaders at companies like Enron, WorldCom and Arthur Anderson. How do you lead teams who are wary of leaders, who are disillusioned by the multitude of examples of hollow leadership? This climate has certainly raised the bar for current and future leaders. People follow the footsteps of those they consider trustworthy. You cannot have effective leadership without credibility; and the quickest route to earn credibility is to act as a Mensch.

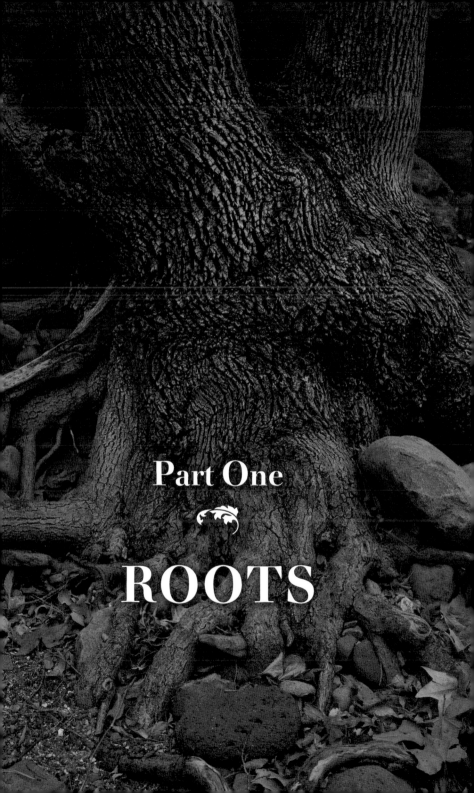

Part One

ROOTS

Chapter One

*"Humility is the foundation of all the other virtues hence,
in the soul in which this virtue does not exist there cannot be
any other virtue except in mere appearance."*
-Saint Augustine-

The Most Beautiful Word in English—*Humility*

Many years ago, one of my university professors mentioned that the word "windowsill" was voted the most beautiful word in the English language. Being an armchair linguist, this factoid naturally stayed with me. Words have enormous power. They can make us erupt into laughter or bring tears to our eyes. They can influence, inspire, manipulate and shock. They can build and destroy. Some words have different effects on different people. One such word is **humility**. It is one of those words that are seldom in neutral gear. Some among us love the word and all it stands for. Some almost fear it and interpret it synonymously with lack of self-confidence or timidity. It is impossible to be a true Mensch without humility. But a Mensch's humility is combined with fierce independence and inner strength. These are part of a Mensch's roots. Buried deep, they are a source of perseverance.

The dictionary defines humility as the quality or state of someone who is modest, who lacks pretense, who does not believe that he or she is superior to others. The word humility first struck me in the context of leadership when Jim Collins mentioned it in his seminal work, *Good to Great: Why Some Companies Make the Leap… and Others Don't*[1]. In this book, Collins examined companies that went from good to great by sustaining 15-year cumulative stock returns at, or below, the general stock market, and after a transition point, cumulative returns at least three times the market over the next 15 years. Among the many characteristics that distinguished these companies from others is that they all had a Level 5 leader. Level 5 leaders direct their ego away from themselves to the larger goal of leading their company to greatness. These leaders are a complex, paradoxical mix of intense professional will and extreme personal humility. They will create superb results but shun public adulation, and are never boastful. They are described as modest. An example of such a leader who epitomized humility is David Packard, the co-founder of Hewlett-Packard, who, in Jim Collins' words, defined himself as an HP man first and a chief executive officer second. He was a man of the people, practicing management by walking around his company and talking openly to his employees. Shunning all manner of publicity, Packard is quoted as saying: "You shouldn't gloat about anything you've done; you ought to keep going and find something better to do."

Another example of a leader with Mensch qualities is the Chief Executive Officer of Enbridge, Patrick Daniel. He espouses two leadership attributes: determination to create results and humility, shifting the focus away from himself and continually recognizing the contributions of others. "I have learned through the lives of great leaders," he said, "that greatness comes from humility and being, at times, self-effacing."[2] Clearly these leaders, and many others like them, don't espouse the meaning of humility as "meek." On the contrary, their humility is the source of their strength. And that's one of the attributes we notice when we are in the presence of a Mensch—a quiet, unassuming strength that is more powerful precisely because it is understated.

But the notion of being self-effacing is one that we struggle with in our competitive culture, prescribing that we take every opportunity to toot our own horn, and that we don't dare leave the house without our dynamic elevator speech all rehearsed. We do often confuse humility with timidity. Humility is not clothing ourselves in an attitude of self-abasement or self-denigration. A Mensch's humility is all about maintaining pride about who he or she is, about achievements and worth—but without arrogance. It is the antithesis of hubris, that excessive, arrogant pride which often leads to the derailment of some corporate heroes, as it does with the downfall of the tragic hero in Greek drama. It's about a quiet confidence without the need for a meretricious selling of one's wares. It's about being content to let others discover the layers of one's talents without having to boast about them. It's a lack of arrogance—not a lack of aggressiveness—in the pursuit of achievement.

A field where arrogance is often rampant is sports. Having a star in that field who exemplifies humility is a rare and shining example. An example of this is Anthony Kevin "Tony" Dungy, former professional American football player, and the current head coach of the Indianapolis Colts of the National Football League. Tony is known for his low-key, humble manner. Those who come in contact with him say that he never talks about himself or his accomplishments, even though he has a long list of accomplishments to his credit. He is one of the two first African American head coaches to make it to the Super Bowl. Mark W. Merrill, of the *Indianapolis Star*, summarized Tony Dungy's humble approach: "Humility does not mean you think less of yourself. It just means you think more of others. That's who Tony Dungy is. Always deflecting the attention and credit to others—his coaches, his players, his father and mother, his wife and children."[3] He is a football coach with a teacher's mentality: instead of shouting and intimidating, he shows players what to do with a quiet dignity and strength. "Tony taught me this lesson, and I think all leaders—politicians, teachers, business managers—can learn from his example."[4]

An interesting dichotomy is that, often, the higher people rise, the more they have accomplished, the higher the humility index. Those who achieve the most, brag the least and the more secure they are in themselves, the more humble they are. "True merit is like a river—the deeper it is, the less noise it makes."[5] We have all come across people like that and feel admiration for them. These are the Mensches who practice humility as a quiet virtue.

There is also the understated humility of everyday people we work with who have the ability to get the job done without drawing attention to themselves. Witness the employee who is working at his computer into the late hours, purely motivated by a keen sense of duty; the executive assistant who stays after 5:30 p.m. on a Friday night in an empty office to await a courier; or the manager who quietly cancels an important personal event to fly out of town to attend to the company's business. This is akin to the philanthropist who gives an anonymous donation.

Humility is also a meta-virtue. It crosses into an array of principles. For example, we can safely declare that there cannot be authenticity without humility. Why? Because, there is always a time in a leader's journey, when one will be in a situation of not having all the answers. Admitting this and seeking others' input requires humility.

Another mark of 'The Leader as a Mensch' is his or her treatment of others. Mensch leaders treat everyone with respect, regardless of position. Years ago, I came across this reference: the sign of a gentleman is how he treats those who can be of absolutely no use to him. This is also a mark of humility.

Something interesting happens, when we approach situations from a perspective of humility—it opens us up to possibilities as we choose open-mindedness and curiosity over protecting our point of view. The Mensch leader spends more time in that wonderful space of the 'beginner's mind,' willing to learn from what others have to offer. This translates into moving away from pushing into allowing, away from insecure to secure, away from seeking approval to seeking enlightenment. It's forgetting about being perfect and enjoying being in the moment.

There are many benefits to practicing humility, to being in a state of non-pretence: it improves relationships across all levels, it reduces anxiety, it encourages more openness and, paradoxically, it enhances one's self-confidence. It opens a window to a higher self. For me, it re-places "windowsill" as the most beautiful word in the English language.

Leaves of Humility

🌿 There are times when swallowing one's pride is particularly difficult and any intentions of humility fly out the window as we get engaged in a contest of perfection, each side seeking to look good. If you find yourself in such no-win situations, consider developing some strategies to ensure that the circumstances don't lead you to lose your grace. Try this sometimes. Just stop talking and allow the other person to be in the limelight. There is something very liberating in this strategy.

🌿 Here are three magical words that will produce more peace of mind than a week at an expensive retreat: "You are right."

🌿 Catch yourself if you benignly slip into preaching or coaching without permission. Is zeal to impose your point of view overtaking discretion? Is your correction of others reflective of your own needs?

🌿 Seek others' input on how you are showing up in your leadership path. Ask, "How am I doing?" It takes humility to ask such a question. And even more humility to consider the answer.

🌿 Encourage the practice of humility in your company through your own example. Each time you share credit for successes with others, you reinforce the ethos for your constituents. Consider mentoring or coaching emerging leaders on this key attribute of leadership.

✤ William Temple, Archbishop of Canterbury, stated: "Humility does not mean thinking less of yourself than of other people, nor does it mean having a low opinion of your own gifts. It means freedom from thinking about yourself at all." If you are in the habit of concentrating mostly on your immediate personal areas of concern, decide to widen your sphere of concern—spend one day a month where you will devote time to considering being outwardly oriented, focusing on the wider perspectives of community and world issues. Perhaps volunteering to bestow some of your talents to others less fortunate, teaching an elderly person computer skills, mentoring younger people, or spending time with terminally ill children.

✤ Make it a habit to ask more questions—in conversations, in meetings, in casual encounters. It's one of the most useful tools for productive conversations and it boosts the self-esteem of the recipients.

✤ Don't attempt to do others' jobs. If someone is struggling with a task, we are sometimes inclined to intervene and take over, or stand behind them and direct, much like a back-seat driver. While we have good intentions, these interventions belittle others. Let the person ask for help, if they so choose.

✤ Those who have humility have a genuine desire to discover what other people think about issues, what their dreams and aspirations are, what they have to offer. Make an effort to cultivate curiosity.

✤ The next time something goes wrong on a project, suspend blame and ask: "What can we learn?"

✤ Hire people who are smarter than you are—whose talents surpass yours—and give them opportunities for growth. It's the smart thing to do and it is a sign of high personal humility.

Chapter Two

"I have come to realize that, for me at least, the quest for 'authenticity' is really a new spin on an age-old quest to find meaning and do the right thing. It's a journey not a destination; a process not an answer."
-Hugh Mason-

The Talisman of Leadership—Authenticity

Just as roots are vital for a tree's growth and health, so is authenticity essential to a leader's survival and development. In his popular book, *Authentic Leadership*, Bill George, Chief Executive Officer of Medtronic, says: "The one essential quality you must have to lead is to be your own person, authentic in every regard."[6] 'The Leader as a Mensch' is the epitome of ***authenticity***. The hallmark of this person is candor—the avoidance of all deception. When we are in the presence of a Mensch, we cannot help but notice the absence of artificiality. We sense that we are confronted with a real person, one who doesn't set out to make an impression. A Mensch just is.

Some time ago, I heard a young woman say, "I am enough." I was struck and intrigued by the expression and so I set out to research it. It originated with Carl Rogers, the psychotherapist, who was asked how he did what he did, so successfully. His response was, "Before a session with a client, I let myself know that 'I am enough'. Not perfect—because perfect wouldn't be enough. But I am human, and there is nothing that this client can say or do or feel that I cannot feel in myself. I can be with them. I am enough."[7] This echoes the serenity of mind, the calm spirit that characterizes a Mensch who doesn't come from a sense of incompleteness, which is so often associated with modern humanity. Quite the contrary—these leaders come from the standpoint of being enough, of seeing themselves as complete human beings, providing a unique contribution to the world by giving their own brand of wisdom, ingenuity, perceptiveness, fairness, and fierce loyalty to their organizations and to those they lead. Perhaps this is what Joseph Campbell meant when he told us that "each of us is a unique creature, and that, if we are ever to give any gift to the world, it will have to come out of our own experience and fulfillment of our potentialities, not someone else's."[8]

A Mensch is a person of integrity, a quality which is defined in the dictionary as "a state of being complete or undivided." So what does this mean in terms of leadership? It means that the leader is complete in his or her devotion to the vision of the organization, to the standards of his or her profession or calling; such leaders are undivided in their sincere commitment to the well-being of those they lead. This also means that these leaders will honor their commitment long after the conditions under which the promise was made, have changed.

Monica Patten, President and Chief Executive Officer of Community Foundations of Canada (CFC), is an example of an authentic leader who lives her values. She puts her money where her mouth is. When she took charge of the CFC in the early 1990s, the organization had less than 30 members. By staying true to her vision, she grew the organization which now oversees 145 community foundations across Canada with assets of $2 billion. In an interview on *Charity Village*, she stated that the traits that make a great leader are compassion, the ability to listen and hear, a solid sense of who one is, and an ability to bring that to life. "It's how you behave. Money and mouth go together. I see and hear, over and over again, people spouting off all these things, but their practices tell you something so different. So for me, it's about alignment with the values, the principles and the behavior."[9] What Patten calls "alignment" is another word for authenticity: A match between what's inside and what's outside.

Authenticity also implies a steadfast commitment to honesty, to being truthful. To that end, consider the notion of the corporate child: we are all a product of our upbringing, and our families of origin were the first organizations that we experienced. This is where we first learned about power, hierarchy, rules of conduct, competition for rewards and avoidance of punishment. This is where we also learned to lie. In a fascinating article by Po Bronson, *New York Magazine*, February 10, 2008, entitled "Learning to Lie," researchers report that "…the most disturbing reason children lie is that parents teach them to… they learn it from us… they see us do it." In longitudinal studies of young children and lying, it was found that children, who are still lying by age seven, are likely to continue the behavior for the rest of their childhood. Other research has found that when adults are asked to keep diaries of their own lies, "they admit to about one lie for every five social interactions, which works out to one per day, on average. The vast majority of these lies are white lies, lies to protect ourselves or others, like telling the guy at work who brought in his wife's muffins that they taste great…" Parents also encourage kids to tell white lies, such as the proper conduct when they open a gift that they don't like. Asked to tell so many white lies and watching their parents do it, "children gradually get comfortable with being disingenuous. Insincerity becomes, literally, a daily occurrence." It is the ethos that some end up bringing to the workplace. I believe it was Peter Senge who said that we tell the truth in organizations up to the level of our embarrassment, up to the level of our paycheck. This is admittedly not an easy situation, but 'The Leader as a Mensch' strives to promote truth telling in the organization. He or she does so by the eloquence of their example. Are you known as a truth teller in your organization?

Part of a Mensch's code of conduct is that they are also promise-keepers. This applies to even the smallest of promises. Years ago, I met the chief executive officer of a Fortune 500 organization. I noticed something about him. He carried with him a small, black notebook into which he noted down any promise he made—no matter how junior the person was to whom he spoke, he made the same effort to note down his promises to that person so that he could follow through. We can rely on the word of such a person. We don't hear the expression 'a gentleman's agreement' as often any more. It refers to an unwritten agreement backed only by the integrity of the individuals involved in the transaction. It is an agreement based on honor, on the premise that the person's word is the pledge. This is one of the sterling qualities of a Mensch and it is based on a firm commitment to authenticity.

Conformity smooths our day's journey at work. Blind conformity, however, has its downsides. It saps creativity for one. It removes all sense of individuality. If you are a leader who demands conformity, I encourage you to think how this might erode your constituents' authenticity as they are pressured to conform. I once worked for a leader in a technology company, who adopted, as part of the company values, the notion of "intelligent disobedience." The concept comes from Seeing Eye dogs. While dogs must learn to obey the commands of the blind person, they must also know when they need to disobey commands that can put the owner in harm's way, such as when a car is approaching. Intelligent disobedience is not about being difficult and disobeying for disobedience sake. Rather, it is about being given the authority to use your judgment—for example, when a decision no longer applies or when a rule interferes with the well-being of the customer. It is, for example, giving authority to the person closest to the customer to make a decision on the spot to right a wrong, even if the decision is contrary to some established rule of the organization. It is essentially obeying the rules unless you have a better idea. The concept of intelligent disobedience was introduced to the corporate arena by Jim Taylor and Watts Wacker in their book, *The Five Hundred Year Delta* and is now entrenched in the culture of successful companies like Microsoft.

A major tenet of 'The Leader as a Mensch' is transparent communication, a by-product of their lucid thinking and uncompromising ethic. They say a great deal with a few words and there is no communication gap between their internal vision of the world and its outward expression. There is directness in their language—we experience it as one might a black and white photograph, where the attention to the subject is not skewed by color. This transparency in communication is the holy grail of leadership, especially today, where a lack of transparency can be particularly detrimental to an organization. As Warren Bennis says in *The Power of Truth*,[10] today, any of your employees can walk out the door and post embarrassing company news on a blog. Witness the Kryptonite Bike Lock debacle that spread over the Internet to thousands of people in a matter of days. The initial blog posting was on Engadget Mobile (and was quickly picked up by dozens of other bloggers); the posting included a video showing Kryptonite brand bicycle locks being opened with ordinary ball-point pens. It was not until *The New York Times* ran a story on the bike lock issue that the company posted a communication on its website.

It is reported that there are currently four million blogs in the blogosphere.[11] If you want to monitor anything that is being said about you, your company or your product, read Steve Rubel's article which details sites, such as PubSub.com that will send you RSS feeds to stay alert to anything that is relevant to your world. Employees are increasingly holding open dialogues on social networking sites such as Facebook, MySpace, Yelp.com, Epinions, Twitter, Digg and so on. These act as viral marketing tools, reaching large audiences around the world in a matter of seconds.

Much has been written about 'CEO disease'—a term that describes the isolation that surrounds a leader when constituents are reluctant to bring bad news or worst-case scenarios to them for fear that such disclosure might trigger a shoot-the-messenger reaction. Establish a culture that values openness—a literal, not only figurative, open door policy. Make it safe for employees to stick their neck out. Consider instituting "Giraffe Awards" to encourage people to stick their necks out for the overall good of the company and its stakeholders.

A fallout of working for, or being associated with, an inauthentic leader is that this person robs us of our own authenticity as we tread carefully around them, playing a slow, cautious chess game. We carefully watch the metrics—we focus on what keeps us safe in our jobs. In the process they don't get the best out of us—they get our labor but not our full engagement—that X factor that divides high performance from minimum acceptable standards. We all know too well that high engagement is one of the keys to building a high-performance, sustainable organization in today's competitive environment. It's what every organization seeks—employees who give their discretionary effort every day, people who go the extra mile to help their organization achieve critical goals. There are many ways to foster that engagement in organizations—one of them is to take a close look at the quality of the leader. Is the leader an authentic person? Do people feel that the leader is who he or she says they are? Does that person engender trust, that is, are people convinced that the leader has no hidden agenda, and that the person genuinely cares for them? All of these factors affect engagement and the bottom line. Lack of authenticity in a leader carries a hefty price tag.

A test of our veracity as leaders is the annual or semi-annual performance reviews. While a necessary aspect of corporate life, these can be instruments of mild torture for those being reviewed. No matter how busy you are with other more pressing business issues, promise yourself to enter those review sessions with the utmost of authenticity. Before you write the first word, sit back and see that person as a real human being. It is very difficult to capture the sum totality of an individual in a form. More animosity and erosion of trust have been unnecessarily generated through the dreaded performance reviews than through any other HR process. A few decades ago, a leader to whom I reported and for whom I had great respect, reviewed my performance and wrote "rarely, if ever late" as the rating for my attendance. When I pointed out that, in fact, I was never late, he said that he couldn't write that, as this might be perceived by head office as the "halo effect" because "no one is never late" and that this would cast doubt on the veracity of all the other comments in the performance reviews. If you are unsure how to rate someone because you have not had a chance to observe them in a certain behavior, level with them and ask their help in rating that particular aspect of their performance instead of guessing. Watch the level of trust soar with that individual.

Authenticity also comes when we focus on one thing, one central thing that truly matters to us. There is a scene in *City Slickers*, the movie, where Jack Palance, the cowboy sage, has a coaching conversation with the green city dweller played by Billy Crystal. Billy's character is plagued by a mid-life crisis, trying to find renewal and a life purpose on a cattle driving vacation. In the scene, Jack Palance asks Billy Crystal: "Do you know what the secret of life is…? One thing, just one thing." When Billy Crystal asks: "What is the one thing?" Jack Palance replies: "That's what you've got to figure out."

What is the 'one thing' that the cowboy sage, raising his index finger, teaches our hero about the meaning of life? It's the one thing that you are devoted to, the one thing that matters to you—in your work as a leader, in your life. This humorous scene echoes the thinking of the great philosopher, Søren Kierkegaard, in his work *Purity of Heart: Is To Will One Thing*. Kierkegaard tells us that it is only by simplifying our life to center on one thing that we can become a whole, integrated authentic person. That "one thing" will differ from person to person but, for all, it is the process of creating a single-life-purpose aimed toward the good.[12] What is the one thing for you in your leadership mission?

Leadership is difficult work and it can be easy to stray from who we are at the core in order to satisfy the business imperatives. Being totally authentic may present particular challenges in today's highly competitive environments where, for example, proprietary knowledge needs to be closely guarded, or where news of impending layoffs need to be managed in order to avoid losing key staff. We can be unwittingly mired in politics. We sometimes find ourselves in situations where we need to continuously look over our shoulder to protect ourselves. We cannot always trust that others are genuine with us. Even with the best of intentions, even when we strive to do our very best, others will sometimes betray us. Much happens in the course of our careers as we climb the achievement ladder and we can sometimes, slowly and imperceptibly, wander off from our authentic selves, the core of who we are. Despite all of this, we need to make every effort to stay true to who we are. Find the way to yourself. Or, as Howard Thurman eloquently said, "Find the grain in your own wood."

Leaves of Authenticity

🌱 Living your values as a leader every day is an important key component of authentic leadership. However, you need to periodically examine these values to consider their validity in today's environment. Examine whether or not they still fit your current reality. Work/life balance, for example, is no longer a perk—it may be an essential requirement for attracting the best minds to your organization.

🌱 Are you in the habit of making hasty promises that you know from past experience you are unable to keep? Think back on what promises you made, to whom, and see if you can fulfill some of these.

🌱 In particular, think twice about promises you make to young people. Breaking those promises are particularly damaging to their views of the world and adults.

🌱 There is a real freedom when we shed all affectation. Are there times in your life when you see yourself being forced to put on a show to make an impression on others? Resolve to stop that, once and for all. Watch yourself soar when you are unencumbered by the weight of pretense.

🌱 Tell yourself, "I am enough"—and mean it.

🌱 Consider reading *The Managerial Moment of Truth: The Essential*

Step in Helping People Improve Performance by Bruce Bodaken and Robert Fritz. The book outlines the concept of truth telling as a way to eradicate bad performance habits early on and to institutionalize good behaviors. The four-step technique to make every performance conversation an authentic and productive dialogue is well worth exploring.

☙ Straight talk, self confidence and simplicity—these are the building blocks of substance, the triumph over image. Think about how you can make these a daily habit.

☙ Are there areas in your life where you might lack consistency without intending to? For example, are you kind to some people but not to others? Are you completely truthful in some circumstances but not in others? What does this insight tell you?

☙ "Hucksters tell great stories. Leaders tell their own stories."[13] Start collecting personal stories that you can use to illustrate to others important aspects of your leadership style, such as, what motivates you to lead; what your philosophy of leading is; and who you are as a person. Personal stories are the most effective form of storytelling for leaders.

☙ Adversity reveals our true character. Consider your conduct when things go wrong. Remind yourself that, as a leader, you are continuously under a looking glass. People want to be inspired by you.

☙ When you are given a script you didn't write for a presentation that you have to deliver, spend extra time to make the words your own. It will pay dividends.

☙ Purge your presentations of inadvertently inflated language that often ends with others questioning our authenticity as a speaker. For example, replace the words "eating establishments" with "restaurants", "learning environments" with "schools" or "universities", "expeditious" with "efficient." Take an inspiration from Winston Churchill who said, "Speak in short, homely words of common usage."

❧ Carl Jung said that there is always the danger that the things we have neglected will return with added force. Does this resonate with you? If so, resolve today to take some action to deal with those issues or people you have forgotten, or left behind. This is another rung on the authenticity ladder.

❧ To understand the connection between authenticity and blogging as the new and different way for businesses to communicate, read *Naked Conversations*, by Robert Scoble and Shel Israel who help run Microsoft's *Channel 9* website. Learn the six pillars of blogging.

❧ Are you forced to live in disharmony between who you are and what you do? Have you turned a deaf ear to the whispers of your heart? Resolve today to take action to start the journey back to finding yourself, to reconnecting with your passions and values. If this is not possible for you because of restrictions in your current circumstance, think about small compromises that you can start making right now to be more in a state of harmony.

❧ If you sometimes think that you are losing yourself in the pressure of situations, consider picking up a copy of Kevin Cashman's *Leadership from the Inside Out*. This timeless classic is more than just another book on leadership—it is an interactive journey that will challenge you to answer three important questions: Who are you? Where are you going? And, why are you going there?

❧ If you are an emergent leader, comfortable with seeking approval before making any decisions, develop a plan to start practicing self-reliance. Start with smaller scale decisions and progressively move on to more significant ones. Only when we free ourselves from the need to have others' approval, can we truly start to evolve into the authentic leaders we were meant to be.

❧ Consider the notion of having a "Noble Goal"—a brief and compelling statement of purpose that would help you evaluate your daily choices. Beyond a mission statement, a Noble Goal incorporates all aspects of your life (personal, family, career, community) and inspires you to live your best life, every day. To help you reflect on and define your Noble Goal, try the exercises in *At The Heart of Leadership: How to Get Results with Emotional Intelligence* by Joshua Freedman.

Chapter Three

"People will forget what you said. People will forget what you did. But people will never forget how you made them feel."
-Maya Angelou-

Ghandi's Neurons—Empathy

While empathy is an emotional activity, it is far from being a sentimental topic. At its core, *empathy* keeps relationships running smoothly. It is one of the prime distinguishing characteristics of a Mensch—an integral part of the deep-seated roots from which spring kindness, compassion, and understanding.

Consider that, fundamentally, leadership is a relationship—a relationship between leaders and followers, between leaders and colleagues, customers and other stakeholders. Without this relationship, leadership simply doesn't exist. If we accept that leadership is the relationship, then empathy is the most crucial component for relationship success.

How we make others feel is the secret to human relationships.

While we must be aware of how others feel, as leaders, we cannot set out to make everybody like us. In fact, the pursuit of being liked as a leader only leads to mediocrity. As former US Secretary of State, General Colin L. Powell put it: "Trying to get everyone to like you is a sign of mediocrity. You'll avoid the tough decisions, you'll avoid confronting the people who need to be confronted, and you'll avoid offering differential rewards based on differential performance because some people might get upset."

So while we cannot control how others feel about us, we can control how others feel about themselves when they interact with us.

'The Leader as a Mensch' has an uncanny ability to make others, no matter what position they occupy in the corporate totem pole, feel respected and valued. When we are in their presence, we sense that they place their focus totally on us for that moment. They have what has been termed 'social generosity.' We invariably walk away from them feeling energized and better about ourselves. This is because they have empathy, the empathy that makes them sense our need to feel important. They see us not as we are but as who we could become. Simply put, they care about how we feel. What a wonderful gift it is, to be able to bestow this on everyone we encounter. This is what we experience as executive presence. One would argue that it is impossible to have executive presence without empathy because a major requirement for executive presence is the ability to connect with others.

The importance of empathy for establishing connection has even been proven neurologically. We now know that medical patients with lesions in the prefrontal-amygdala circuits that support the expression of empathy show significant deficits in relationship skills, even though their cognitive abilities remain intact.[14]

There are numerous studies that link empathy to achieving business success. They include studies that correlate empathy with increased sales, with the performance of best managers of product development teams and with enhanced performance in an increasingly diverse workforce.[15] Increasingly, the topic of empathy is encroaching in the business world. We are now even seeing terms such as empathy marketing, empathy selling and user empathy which refers to user interface. Indeed, empathy is valued currency in any leadership role. It allows us to create bonds of trust; it sharpens our 'people acumen' by giving us insights into what others may be feeling or thinking; it helps us understand how or why others are reacting to situations, and it informs our decisions. This all leads to being more effective as a leader.

A formal definition of empathy is the ability to identify and understand another's situation, feelings, and motives—the capacity to recognize other peoples' concerns. The metaphor language for empathy includes "putting yourself in the other person's shoes" or "seeing things through someone else's eyes." This capacity is particularly critical to leadership development in our new zeitgeist of young, independent, highly marketable and mobile workers. In a now widely-read *Harvard Business Review* article entitled, "What Makes a Leader?" by Dr. Daniel Goleman (November-December 1998), Goleman isolates three reasons for empathy: the increasing use of teams (which he refers to as "cauldrons of bubbling emotions"), the rapid pace of globalization (with cross-cultural dialogues easily leading to misunderstandings) and the growing need to retain talent. "Leaders with empathy," states Dr. Goleman, "do more than sympathize with people around them: they use their knowledge to improve their companies in subtle, but important ways." This doesn't mean that they agree with everyone's view or try to please everybody. Rather, they "thoughtfully consider employees' feelings—along with other factors—in the process of making intelligent decisions."

Along those lines, in his book *A Whole New Mind: Moving from the Information Age to the Conceptual Age,* Daniel Pink predicts that power will reside with those who have strong right-brain qualities. In order to compete in the new economy market, the author prescribes six areas that are vital to our success. One of these six areas or "senses" (as he calls them) is empathy, the ability to imagine yourself in someone else's position and to intuit what they are feeling, to understand what makes people tick, to create relationships and to be caring of others. This sense is very difficult to outsource or automate and increasingly important to business.

Empathy, then, is an ability that is well-worth cultivating. It's a soft, abstract tool in a leader's toolkit that leads to hard, tangible results. But where does empathy come from? Is it a cognitive or affective process? From my perspective, I believe that we need to use our cognitive ability to understand another person's thoughts, feelings, reactions, concerns, and motives. This means truly making an effort to stop and think for a moment about the other person's perspective in order to begin to understand where they are coming from. And then we need the emotional capacity to care for that person's concern. Caring does not mean that we would always agree with that person—that we would change our position—but it does mean that we would be in tune with what that person is going through so that we can respond in a manner that acknowledges their thoughts, feelings or concerns.

Scientists have discovered mirror neurons, a type of brain cells, also dubbed Ghandi's Neurons. When we witness emotion in someone else, for example, the neurons that 'fire up' in our own brain are the same neurons that would become active should we feel that emotion. This discovery explains our ability to understand others' intentions and mental states as well our capacity to feel empathy. There is no doubt that we are hard-wired for empathy. The presence of mirror neurons is the scientific mechanism that allows us to walk in another person's shoes, to feel another's pain. Science has given us new proof about our capacity as humans to understand each other, to connect and to bond.[16]

This capacity is expressed in its highest form by 'The Leader as a Mensch' who can easily forge positive connections with others. Some of these leaders are what David West Keirsey calls "idealists"—people who use empathy to engender trust and build bonds, who act as catalysts able to create positive communities for the greater good. These people provide inspiration for the rest of us. They show us the way forward. Examples of idealists are Mohandas Karamchand Ghandi and Anna Eleanor Roosevelt. A current example of an idealist is Mary Therese Winifred Robinson, former President of Ireland and subsequently High Commissioner for Human Rights at the United Nations. Robinson is a living example of an empathetic leader who, halfway through her term in office, had reached an unheard-of popularity rating of 93 percent. She devoted her entire life to fighting for human rights, both in Ireland and in the world. A famous incident involves her visit to Rwanda where she called attention to the atrocities of the war in that country. During a speech at a press conference following her visit to Rwanda, she became visibly emotional. As a lawyer trained to be rational, she was angry at herself for not being able to manage her emotions. Vincent Browne, editor of *The Sunday Tribune* passed her a note at the end of the press conference saying simply, "You were magnificent."[17]

Years ago, I came across a saying that went something like 'the measure of a man (or woman) is how they treat someone who is of absolutely no use to them.' Empathy should not be selective. It should be a daily habit.

Leaves of Empathy

🌿 Listen, truly listen to people. Listen with your ears, eyes, and to the hidden emotions behind what they are saying to you, to contextual aspects.

🌿 Don't interrupt people. Don't dismiss their concerns offhand. Don't rush to give advice. Don't change the subject. Allow people their moment.

🌿 Increase your ability to understand others' non-verbal communication because often people don't communicate openly what they think or feel. To that end, consider Dr. Paul Ekman's *Emotions Revealed: Recognizing Faces and Feelings to Improve Communication and Emotional Life.* Professor of Psychology, University of California, San Francisco Medical School, Ekman spent over 40 years studying emotion and facial expression.

🌿 Practice *"The 93 Percent Rule"*. We know from the famous study by Albert Mehrabian, Professor Emeritus of Psychology, University of California, Los Angeles, that words—the things we say—account for only 7 percent of the total message that people receive. The other 93 percent of the message that we communicate when we speak is contained in our tone of voice and body language. It's important, then, to spend some time to understand how we come across when we communicate with others. A simple act like frowning, or a raised eyebrow when someone is explaining their point of view, can disconnect us from the speaker and make us appear as though we lack understanding.

❧ Use people's names. Remember the names of people's spouse and children so that you can refer to them more personally.

❧ Be fully present when you are with people. Don't check your email, look at your watch or take phone calls when a direct report drops into your office to talk to you. Put yourself in their shoes. How would you feel if your boss did that to you?

❧ Smile at people.

❧ Encourage people, particularly the quiet ones, when they speak up in meetings. A simple thing like an attentive nod can boost someone's confidence.

❧ As James M. Kouzes and Barry Z. Posner say: "Encourage the heart." Pay attention to what people are doing and catch them doing the right things. Give genuine recognition.

❧ When you give praise, spend a little effort to make your genuine words memorable for your constituents: "You are an asset to this team because…"; "This was pure genius."; "I would have missed this if you hadn't picked it up."

❧ Show people that you care by taking a personal interest in them. Show genuine curiosity about their lives. Ask questions about their hobbies, their challenges, their families, their aspirations.

❧ Spend time with the people who work for you. Get out from behind your desk and walk around and meet them on their turf. We have often been told not to rely solely on email as a form of communication. To that end, read "The Human Moment at Work" by Edward M. Hallowell, a *Harvard Business Review* article (January 1, 1999) mentioned in James M. Kouzes and Barry Z. Posner's *The Leadership Challenge: How to Get Extraordinary Things Done in Organizations.*

❧ When you visit one of your subordinates' offices, don't stand while you talk to them. Sit down for a moment so that you are both at the same level while you are talking.

❧ Have your finger on the pulse of your department or organization. Learn how to read the mood of a group.

❧ Be sensitive to diversity. Make a substantial effort to understand constituents of different cultures.

❧ Read a good book on Emotional Intelligence (EI) or Emotional Quotient (EQ). Better still, attend a workshop on it; consider hiring a coach.

❧ As much as you can, hire people who are empathetic.

❧ As a leader, you have a unique opportunity to touch lives deeply. Once in a while, remind yourself of this awesome responsibility.

❧ When you meet someone for the first time, make a conscious effort to focus on how they are feeling about themselves in your presence.

❧ Resolve to be curious. Treat your conversation as an opportunity to discover 'what makes this person tick'.

❧ There are many emotional intelligence tests that can give you valuable feedback on your empathy quotient. These include the *Six Seconds Emotional Intelligence Assessment (SEI),* the *Emotional Competence Inventory (ECI),* the *Mayer-Salovey-Caruso Emotional Intelligence Test (MSCEIT),* and the *Emotional Quotient Inventory (Bar-On EQ-i).*

Part Two

TRUNK

Chapter Four

"Every person's work, whether it be literature or music or pictures or architecture or anything else, is always a portrait of that person."
-Samuel Butler-

I Swear by Apollo—Accountability

"I swear by Apollo"… so starts the *Oath of Hippocrates*, an oath of ethical, professional behavior sworn by all new physicians—a promise to practice good medicine to the best of their ability, for the good of their patients. It essentially boils down to a commitment to "do no harm." If there is one motto that defines a Mench's ethos, it is surely this one. In fact, one of the definitions of Mensch is to be "an upstanding person who takes responsibility for his or her actions." It is so much a part of what defines a Mensch, that, continuing our tree metaphor, it represents the tree's trunk—its main structural, most stable and visible part; akin to the consistent *accountability* shown by 'The Leader as a Mensch' at every encounter or undertaking. 'Doing no harm' is what drives his or her accountability at all times.

Wouldn't it be great to have such an oath for all leaders—an oath of personal accountability, not just for business outcomes and for leading others, but for leading oneself? I am reminded of the biblical proverb: Physician, heal thyself. It suggests that one should take care of one's own faults first before correcting the faults of others. I add to the above: Leader, heal thyself.

Leaders who practice accountability rise above the rest of the crowd. They are noticed. In 2008, a Toronto Maple Leaf Foods plant was found to be implicated in an outbreak of a foodborne illness. Michael McCain, the firm's Chief Executive Officer, immediately took full responsibility. "Certainly knowing that there is a desire to assign blame, I want to reiterate that the buck stops right here… our best efforts failed, not the regulators or the Canadian food safety system… I emphasize: this is our accountability and it's ours to fix, which we are taking on fully."[18]

Any nuts-and-bolts leadership primer will explain that a key leadership competency is also holding others accountable—which entails, among other things, setting clear expectations and guidelines, clearly communicating goals and objectives, following up to ensure fulfillment of responsibilities, providing feedback on performance, coaching those whose performance is not up to par and, finally, taking any necessary corrective action. But a leader cannot expect to successfully hold others accountable if they are not holding themselves accountable first.

While fostering accountability is an important dimension of leadership, it is easy for a leader to slip when it comes to accountability for his or her own behaviors. This can happen even to leaders who do a great job of holding themselves accountable on the big-ticket items—for example, driving for results, whether in sales, operations, marketing or financing; identifying root causes for business problems; developing a vision and strategy; and managing resources effectively.

Let's clarify something before we proceed: no leader worth his salt wakes up in the morning deciding that he or she is 'not going to be accountable today.' No one wants to do a bad job. But things happen during the course of the day that can divert the best of us from our good intentions and, more often than not, those things are unintentional. It is these seemingly innocuous personal slips that I would like to talk about. They take many subtle forms. Let's explore a few of the garden-variety ones:

- Let's say you have a chronic problem employee. Instead of

making the tough decision to let that individual go (because you are a nice person) and after much deliberation and agony, you decide to transfer the person to another department— essentially moving the problem to another part of the company and hoping it will go away. Deep down your intuition is whispering to you that the problem will not just go away. But, in your elation at having found 'the solution' to a nagging problem, you suppress your intuition and come to the office the next day with a spring in your step and a song in your heart relieved at having shed a burden off your shoulders.

- A senior member of your team has a habit of treating lower-ranked individuals very poorly in meetings—interrupting them, discounting their contributions and, generally, exhibiting bad behavior. It mortifies the recipients, embarrasses other team members and even bothers you. Again, because you value harmony and hate confrontation of any kind, you reluctantly choose to ignore the offending behavior and hope that it will stop on its own. The fact that the perpetuator is an aggressive high achiever, successfully delivering results, makes it even harder for you to step up and do something.

- You have just announced the company's drastic cost-cutting measures and asked for everyone in your department to co-operate by eliminating all discretionary spending for a while to help the organization ride out a difficult period. You delivered a genuinely inspiring speech to your team and everyone is on board to make this work. Two days later, employees see a $1,000 chair delivered to your office—an earlier purchase you had genuinely forgotten to cancel. Others, of course, don't judge us by our intentions—they only have the appearance of events to judge us by.

- A mistake was made, the ownership of which falls on several shoulders, including yours. Driven by the anxiety and chaos that ensues, you minimize your role in the fracas, and even unwittingly suffer from temporary corporate amnesia (forgetting that you were fully briefed in advance and setting out to find a scapegoat), genuinely convincing yourself that it is surely someone else's fault. This can easily happen in times of stress because, as a leader, you handle dozens of issues on a daily basis. However, others involved only handle a few issues and remember the course of events with laser-like precision.

Well, the list could go on. Some slips are due to personality preferences, others just from the sheer amount of work and stress that leaders can easily experience. The reasons are multiple and really not important. It's the behaviors that are important. They are all examples of behaviors you would not condone in others when you hold them accountable. And as we all know that when there is a disparity between what you tell others to do and what you do yourself, people will believe your actions and not your words. The fallout of this scenario is an erosion of trust, one of the high prices we pay for lack of self-accountability.

Let's also not neglect to mention that being in a leadership position is not necessarily being in a popular spot. Doing anything can ipso facto elicit criticism. You are always in a fishbowl.

Self-accountability, then, is staying true to ourselves despite difficult circumstances. It's doing the right thing even when we are tempted to bend a few rules for expediency's sake. Perhaps Deborah Lee puts it best: "Self-accountability is who you are when no one is looking." It's also the best anti-dote to feeling victimized by circumstances and, in so doing, frees up precious creative energy for us to accomplish what matters to us. Above all, it entails owning up to the consequences of our decisions and choices, because there is no choice without accountability. This is eloquently explained in a poem from an unknown source:

Choice and Accountability

Feel me. I am your freedom.
I am your wrong decision and hard consequence,
But then I am your sacrifice and your rich blessings.
Your knowledge needs me to grow.
I am the reason you have knowledge.
I am responsibility.
I am the freedom and justice.
I hold wisdom and foolishness,
Truth and untruth,
And the difference between them.
There are two parts to me.
One part cannot exist without the other.
I am a pattern, consistent and strong.
You experience me all throughout your life.
You need me to learn.
I will teach you if you pay attention.
I am your Choice and Accountability.

Leaves of Accountability

 Just as companies are rightfully concerned about how they are viewed by customers or shareholders, consider taking time to reflect on how your actions are viewed by all stakeholders: your direct reports, your peers, your clients. Go through a formal 360 Leadership Assessment process or simply get hold of a leadership assessment form and use it to reflect on how others in your team would rate you on each dimension. Examples include: 'Puts the interests of the team before own interests; Shares credit for successes; Readily shares relevant information; Asks how I am doing; Treats others with respect regardless of their position; Fosters teamwork across all departments; Stands behind decisions made by the team; Provides honest feedback on a timely basis.' (How would others respond to these questions about you?)

 At the end of each day, when you clear your desk before you head home, take a few short minutes to mentally go over your day. Think about significant conversations you held, meetings you attended, emails you sent and other actions you undertook. Are you proud? Could you have done better? This will inspire you to plan your next day around your highest purpose. Getting into this habit of introspection will pay dividends in the long run.

🦢 Decide to hold yourself accountable for developing other leaders. By mentoring a protégé to enhance their personal and professional growth, you strengthen your own leadership skills and reinforce your determination to be self-accountable as you become the model.

🦢 Form a closer alliance with your human resources people— leverage their expertise in human relations and seek their advice on the more puzzling 'people issues' that could derail you from your best intentions.

🦢 Is there an area in your leadership where you may have inadvertently slipped? Should you take steps to rectify this? Consider Tom Peters' "Tip #8" in *100 Ways to Succeed*—If you foul up, fess up, fast and fastidiously (tell the whole truth). And then get on with your life.[19]

🦢 Be self-accountable for your own happiness. No one can go on a diet for you, just as no one can be responsible for your state of mind. We are totally responsible for the impact that others have on us. Spend time to understand the disruptive effect that emotions can have on your behavior and resolve to do something about it.

🦢 When something goes wrong, look inwardly for solutions. It is especially in difficult times that our self-accountability is challenged. Reverend Martin Luther King Jr. said it poignantly: "The ultimate measure of a man is not where he stands in moments of comfort and convenience, but where he stands at times of challenge and controversy."

🦢 When a mistake is made, do you ask "Whose fault is it?" or do you ask "What can we learn from this?" as well as "What can I do to improve this situation?" Consider reading John G. Miller's book *QBQ! The Question behind the Question: Practicing Personal Account-*

ability in Work and in Life. Reading the book inspires one to move away from the blame game we have all been tempted to play at one time or other and take ownership of issues.

🕊 Think about promises you make to new hires during the interviewing courtship period. In our zeal to want to attract the brightest and most talented, we can easily over promise. Keep a record of your interview notes and what you promised to candidates. If subsequent events make it impossible to keep the promises, at least you can address them with the individual. This is better than forgetting about them altogether.

🕊 What about promises you made to yourself? Write out your personal and professional goals with clear targets. Read them once a week. Are your day-to-day actions aligned with your values, your standards, and your philosophy of leading? What are your boundaries? Do you take measures to protect them? If your answers to these questions are negative, what is causing this? What insights does this give you? Use this information as a means to spur you to action rather than guilt.

🕊 In that vein, consider how easy it is for us to slip into neglecting our intimate self when we embark on the leadership journey. On a scale of one to ten, with ten being the highest, where would you score yourself on your ability to monitor and grow your physical, psychological and spiritual dimensions? Do you approach these three key areas with the same careful analysis you devote to the components of your Profit and Loss Statement?

🕊 Molière, the 17th century French dramatist, said, "It is not only what we do, but also what we do not do, for which we are accountable." Is there anything that you are avoiding doing that needs to be done?

For example, are you putting off a difficult conversation? Are you delaying any important decisions? Are you delegating away responsibilities that should stay in your court?

❧ Your organization's vision and values are espoused by management and other senior leaders and managers who keep the vision alive within their staff. However, those further down the organization's hierarchy, who may be reporting to a junior supervisor or team lead, may sometimes experience a different atmosphere. The may be reporting to someone who doesn't live the values and vision but these individuals are too far removed and have no voice. They might as well be working in a different company altogether. You have a responsibility, as a leader, to ensure that all those in your unit, no matter how far down they are in the hierarchy, experience the same values and vision. Don't forget the people in the back rows.

❧ When you hear, "We should do this" in a meeting, ask, "Who will do this?" Ideas captured on a flipchart or whiteboard end up staying there. Have someone record these and determine who will take ownership, what the desired outcomes are, and establish a time frame for achieving the desired results.

❧ I used to work for a leader who established a monthly balance score card for himself and his team. At monthly meetings, he would give himself a pass or fail on each line item and required other team members to rate themselves with the same pass or fail criteria.

❧ When you have evidence that a direct report is in danger of failing in accomplishing his or her goals, step in and offer remedial action. Coach them or assign a coach. Give them the support they need to succeed before it is too late. It's the leader's way.

❧ Help junior members of your team to learn how to set goals and be accountable. Consider making available for them a goal set-ting software such as Success Studios Corporation's GoalPro. The product creates a graphic overview of your goals, and provides action planning management ability; reports and graphs for monitoring purposes; a daily journal for documenting success efforts; a scratch-pad for brainstorming sessions; and a personal success coach feature for encouraging specific actions on a daily basis.[20]

~✦ Meetings, and especially retreats and other annual get-together events, are notorious for generating many ideas but, more often than not, many of these ideas are not revisited. They end up being just talk at the meeting. Resolve to ensure that there is a follow-up and that those who propose favorable ideas are accountable for taking what-ever action is necessary to see the ideas come to fruition.

~✦ Resolve to do no harm in anything that you undertake. If you are certain that you don't have the competence to take on something that is offered, consider that you might be doing harm to someone by accepting it anyway.

Chapter Five

"Part of being optimistic is keeping one's head pointed toward the sun, and one's feet moving forward."
-Nelson Rolihlahla Mandela-

The Leader's Lantern—Optimism

Among the topics that young people study to prepare them for the workforce is calculus, the mathematics of change and motion. While training in calculus is undoubtedly important, I believe that training in *optimism* is also important. Just as it is crucial to solve problems like the velocity of a car at a certain moment in time, it is also crucial to figure out what drives people to give us the very best that they have to offer. Ironically, Gottfried Wilhelm Leibniz, one of the inventors of calculus, is also known for his philosophy of optimism. He was considered to be an inveterate optimist, asserting that we live "in the best of all possible worlds." In the workplace, optimism is an emotional competence that can help boost productivity, enhance employee morale, overcome conflict and have a positive impact on the bottom line.

In writing about optimism, one faces the danger of being seen as advocating a Pollyanna or Quixotic approach. The truth, however, is that optimism has been proven to be a powerful tool that will pay dividends in your personal life and give you a competitive advantage professionally. There is a lot to be gained, indeed, in cultivating an optimistic outlook. Nowhere is optimism, perhaps, more important than in the leading organizations.

A Mensch is an optimist and a purveyor of hope for others. As a leader, he or she creates the conditions that allow others to discover their greatest potential. Highly effective leaders have a transforming effect on their constituents. Among the behavioral indicators of their transformational leadership[21] style, is the ability to convince others that they are capable of achieving levels of performance beyond what they thought possible. They are able to paint an optimistic and attainable view of the future for their followers. They move others from being stuck in the status quo—how things are done around here—and help them see how things could be done better. This concept is echoed in "The Leadership Advantage," an essay in the Drucker Foundations' *On Mission and Leadership: A Leader to Leader Guide* in which Warren Bennis tells us that constituents need these things from their leaders in order to achieve positive results: meaning (or direction); trust (both in the leader and by the leader); a sense of hope and optimism; and results. Such a leader instills confidence that things will always work out. Confidence and optimism impacts others in a very positive way. Every "exemplary leader that I have met," said Bennis, "has what seems to be an unwarranted degree of optimism—and that helps generate the energy and commitment necessary to achieve results."

Consider, as well, the obverse: the effect that pessimistic individuals can have on an organization's creativity and innovation. To be innovative, one needs to be open to new ideas, wide open to seeing possibilities, willing to take risks and encourage others to take risks—willing to challenge the process in order to create new solutions or products or improve processes. In short, one needs to have a sense of adventure and an expectation of success. How can someone who has a pessimistic outlook embrace change over the safety of the known? Those who have a pessimistic outlook typically approach changes to the status quo with the familiar "we tried this before… it won't work… it will never fly." (Such individuals often label themselves as 'devil's advocates.') The negative effect this can have on creativity, innovation, and change is reflected in the title of a new book by Tom Kelley of IDEO, the world's leading design firm: *The Ten Faces of Innovation: IDEO's Strategies for Defeating the Devil's Advocate and Driving Creativity Throughout Your Organization*. Kelley provides a roadmap for those who want to fuel innovative thinking and neutralize the pessimistic, often destructive naysayers who shoot down ideas and stifle creativity. The recipe involves adding ten positive roles or personas to a team, including the Experimenters (who try something new), the Hurdlers (who instantly look for ways to overcome limits and challenges of a situation), and the Collaborators (who bring people together and get things done). I am reminded of a Chinese proverb which says: "The person who says it cannot be done should not interrupt the person doing it."

There are other areas which are impacted positively by optimism. Let's look at sales, for example. A study shows that new sales personnel at Metropolitan Life who scored high on a test for optimism sold 37 percent more life insurance in their first two years than did pessimists.[22] In another study involving debt collectors in a large collection agency, the most successful collectors had significantly higher scores in the area of self-actualization, independence, and optimism.[23] Optimists also receive higher performance scores from their superiors.[24]

There are many examples of the power of optimism in business. Take Ron Johnson, former Vice President and General Manager for Target's Home Décor. He passionately believed in having a culture of optimism, one that encouraged new ideas and innovation. When a new idea was presented to him, he was known for responding with "why not?" as opposed to "why?", which often kills ideas at inception.[25] Optimism is an important ingredient in a leader's arsenal.

Perhaps even more significant are the countless studies that have shown that those who have an optimistic outlook have healthier relationships, enjoy better mental and physical health and live longer. In *The Wisdom of the Ego*, Dr. George E. Vaillant, Professor of Psychiatry at Harvard Medical School, writes about individuals who have "both the capacity to be bent without breaking and the capacity, once bent, to spring back". Vaillant mentions that, in addition to external sources of resilience (such as good health, social supports), these individuals have important internal sources which include a healthy self-esteem, as well as optimism and mature ego defenses. These mature ego defenses (or coping mechanisms) are fully explored in Dr. Vaillant's subsequent book, *Aging Well: Surprising Guideposts to a Happier Life from the Landmark Harvard Study of Adult Development*, a truly fascinating study that will be particularly interesting to fellow boomers. This is a compendium of three different longitudinal studies involving over 800 individuals—men and women, rich and poor—who were followed for more than 50 years, from adolescence to old age. We discover that one of the most powerful predictors of successful aging is habitually using mature coping mechanisms or defenses, what Vaillant calls the ability to "make lemonade out of life's lemons." Vaillant's study discovered five of these coping mechanisms: they are Altruism (doing for others what they need, not what we want to do for them), Sublimation (diverting energy to more constructive pursuits such as creativity, art, sports); Suppression (postponement of stressors, not repression); Humor, and Anticipation. Anticipation is realistic, hopeful planning for the future. This means not operating in a pessimistic crisis mode but preparing and adapting for whatever life brings.

So how does one recognize an optimist? Alan Loy McGinnis, author of *The Power of Optimism*, studied the biographies of over 1000 famous people and isolated 12 characteristics of the optimistic personality. Among these are: optimists look for partial solutions, that is, freed from the tyranny of perfectionism, from paralysis by analysis, they are open to taking small steps towards achieving success. Another characteristic of an optimist McGinnis notes is that they use their imagination to rehearse success—in other words, they play positive mental videos of preferred outcomes, much like sports figures do. (Michael Jordan, for example, once stated that he never plays a game that he hasn't first visualized.) Further, optimists believe that their personal best is yet to come.

This takes us to a researcher who has probably devoted the most time to studying the traits of optimists, Dr. Martin E. P. Seligman, the modern scholar most often associated with the topic. Seligman, former President of the American Psychological Association and Professor of Psychology at the University of Pennsylvania, has devoted decades to studying optimistic people and reports three traits that they have in common: They view adversity in their lives as temporary, specific (not permeating all other aspects of their life), external, not entirely their fault—as opposed to pessimists who view adversity in their lives as permanent (unchangeable), pervasive (affecting all aspects of their life), and personal (viewing themselves as the source of the adversity, i.e., 'all' their fault). In the face of setbacks, challenges or difficult jobs, pessimists are more likely to do worse than predicted and even give up, while optimists will persevere. Optimism, therefore, is also an important component of achievement, and is especially important in times of chaos, change, and turbulence. Those who have an optimistic outlook will roll with the punches, will be more proactive and persistent, and will not abandon hope.

So, where does optimism come from? Is it something we are born with or is it learned? For some lucky individuals, being optimistic comes naturally. The good news is that, for those who don't have it naturally, optimism is an attitude that can be learned and practiced. Watch the Mensches around you. These leaders know that they are the focal point in their organization, in their units—and they understand the responsibility that comes with that position. There is an element of stoicism in their behavior; the absence of complaining. They have no tolerance for mindless complaints—complaints that don't focus on the greater purpose of the organization and its people. They will confront us to think big, act big, and be big. These are the leaders that continually push us to focus on the solution to an issue, rather than becoming trapped by the obstacle. These leaders are genuinely enthusiastic and passionate about their company's vision, their product, and the people who do the work. The enthusiasm is palpable and, if we are fortunate to spend enough time in their presence, it is contagious.

This chapter would not be balanced if we did not address the benefits of pessimism. Pessimists may be more realistic and accurate about potential dangers and pitfalls. At times, when there is a risk of serious negative consequences, a cautious, risk-avoiding evaluation is appropriate and desirable. 'The Leader as a Mensch' feels strongly the weight of this responsibility, the responsibility to exercise good judgment in all decisions. But, even throughout difficulties, they never let us lose the fundamental hope that a group of highly committed people can solve issues and achieve great things. They always point our gaze to the proverbial light at the end of the tunnel.

As research has proven, the positive effects of being optimistic—fighting depression; aiding in professional, academic, and sports achievement; and boosting mental and physical health—outweigh the benefits of being a career pessimist. So how does one balance optimism with difficult times? The answer is, as Seligman explains, "flexible optimism", i.e., having the wisdom to assess situations and identify those that require a pessimistic inquisition and those that call for optimism, for having a "can do attitude." If your default mode is skepticism and pessimism, I strongly encourage you to consider that there might be a huge payoff by including optimism as part of your operating mode. Sir Winston Churchill had a reason for saying: "A pessimist sees the difficulty in every opportunity; an optimist sees the opportunity in every difficulty." Practice seeing the opportunity. Practice having an 'appreciative mind.'

Leaves of Optimism

✒ Avoid negative environments. If this is not realistic, make every effort to seek the company of positive individuals in your organization. Sometimes this may mean fraternizing with peers in other departments. Stay away from the professional complainer. (Be aware that there is a strong connection between pessimism and depression. Research shows that pessimists are four to eight times more likely to succumb to depression.)

✒ The key to high achievement and happiness is to play out your strengths, not correct your weaknesses (Dr. Martin E. P. Seligman). Focus on what you do well. Celebrate your strengths. (If you are not sure what your signature strengths are, consider reading *Now, Discover Your Strengths* by Marcus Buckingham. The book provides you with a web-based interactive feature that allows you to complete a questionnaire developed by the Gallup Organization and discover your own Top-Five Inborn Talents).

✒ Consider taking *Dr. Martin E. P. Seligman's Optimism Test* which is free online at http://www.authentichappiness.org.[26]

✒ Take care of your spiritual and emotional well being by reading inspirational material on a daily basis. This may be different for each person. Some may be inspired by daily quotations, others by reading biographies of successful people in their field and yet others may derive inspiration from reading about innovations. A useful website for keeping up with new inventions is http://www.worldfuturesociety.com.

❧ When faced with setbacks, identify what you can change and proactively try to find ways to do something about it. Manage or ignore what you cannot change. We have often heard this advice—it bears repeating. Be inspired by Benjamin Franklin's words, "While we may not be able to control all that happens to us, we can control what happens inside us."

❧ If you are serious about developing greater optimism, there is no better book than *Learned Optimism: How to Change Your Mind and Your Life* by Dr. Martin E. P. Seligman. Learn his *ABCDE Model* for disputing pessimistic thoughts. This is a very useful and power-ful tool for changing your 'attributional' style (the way you explain events) from pessimistic to optimistic. The tool encourages you to analyze an event that troubles you by following these steps:

A—Adversity: Identify and articulate the adversity.

B—Beliefs: Identify the belief(s) about the adversity. For example, you might make an unsuccessful cold call and then think: I am *never* good at cold calling.

C—Consequences: How do you feel as a result of this belief?

D—Disputation: Dispute your belief. Ask what evidence do I have to support this belief? What are all the possible explanations for the adversity? For example, did you catch the client at an inopportune moment? Was the client distracted by other issues?

E—Energization: List your thoughts and feelings as a result of disputing your negative attribution. You are likely to feel better and this may have a positive effect on your subsequent actions.

Using this tool on a regular basis—getting used to disputing your negative beliefs, essentially arguing with yourself—over time, will result in your positive explanatory style becoming automatic. It is important to note here that this is not about blindly practicing positive thinking. Rather it is about getting into the habit of thinking non-negatively.

↬ Another helpful tool is reframing—deliberately shifting perspective and looking for the hidden positive in a negative situation; the proverbial silver lining. Look for the gift in the adversity.

↬ Consider how a simple shift in the language you use can make a difference in your outlook. In a conversation with a client a few years ago, the words "dropped out" kept surfacing. When the client was encouraged to change the words to "took a hiatus," there was an immediate shift to the positive which was more reflective of the reality of the situation. On the subject of language, do you frequently say: "yes, but" in response to your constituents' suggestions? The "but" automatically negates anything you have said in the beginning part of the sentence. A simple shift to "yes, and…" might make a positive difference in how the message is received. Do a forensic analysis of emails you have sent. Count the proportion of negative to positive words. It could be enlightening.

↬ Become aware of your stance in business meetings. Are you known as the devil's advocate—the one who is quick to shoot down others' ideas? Jumping in too quickly to negate an idea can derail the creative process of others. Often valuable ideas are the result of an initial 'crazy' thought. At meetings, even when we don't have the floor, we are under a magnifying glass. Practice being more upbeat and see what happens. Practice being the last one to speak and see what happens. A primer for brainstorming savvy is a book mentioned before, *The Art of Innovation: Lessons in Creativity from IDEO,*

America's Leading Design Firm by Tom Kelley et al.

🐦 If you run meetings, watch, in particular, situations where a constituent or colleague makes a suggestion and someone else jumps in with another comment. What happens to the first person's comments? Typically, they are ignored as the discussion moves on. This is particularly difficult for the more reticent participant. You can boost their confidence and participation by encouraging them. Stating, for example, that : "Janet made a suggestion earlier that we didn't address," models the way for others.

🐦 When you encounter adversity, ask yourself if this situation will last for your entire life.

🐦 Focus outside of yourself—on important people in your life, on pursuits and projects that fire you up. Bertrand Russell once said that the quickest way to make ourselves miserable is to continually focus on ourselves. His focus on his love of mathematics prevented him from committing suicide.

🐦 Cultivate spontaneity. Consider putting aside all your plans once in a while to take a walk with your kids, play a game or catch a show. Getting out of your comfort zone by being spontaneous helps to develop your optimistic muscle, as spontaneity essentially involves an expectation of having a pleasurable experience.

🐦 If you have teenaged children, encourage them to be aware of the pessimistic phrases they use. Challenge them to develop a more positive outlook. It will be one of your greatest gifts.

🐦 If you need extra motivation for practicing optimism, consider the statistics linking optimism to greater health. As Dr. Martin E. P. Seligman explains, there is evidence to believe that the immune system among optimistic people is stronger than among pessimists.

Optimists also have lower rates of infectious illnesses. Additionally, the probability of death from a second heart attack has been found to be lower in the optimist set.

☙ Read Jon Gordon's *The No Complaining Rule: Positive Ways to Deal with Negativity at Work*. In it, he outlines three practical rules that stand the test of time.

☙ If you are in charge of other people at work, nurture a culture of optimism. Expect people to succeed. Even when they occasionally fail to achieve what they set out to do, encourage them so that they can tackle the next challenge. A simple, "I know you'll do better the next time" can have very positive effects.

☙ Make a point of studying and becoming aware of the ten cognitive distortions, i.e., the ten common mistakes in thinking. Mental Filter (picking out a single negative detail and dwelling on it exclusively so that your vision of reality becomes darkened like the drop of ink that discolors the entire beaker of water) is one of those mistakes as is Emotional Reasoning (assuming your negative emotions necessarily reflect the way things are, i.e., "I feel it, therefore it must be true."). These and the other eight distortions are illustrated in Dr. David D. Burns' seminal book entitled *Feeling Good: The New Mood Therapy*. Analyzing your thoughts to catch yourself when you practice these cognitive distortions in every day events will help you in your quest towards increasing optimism.

Chapter Six

"Quality is never an accident;
it is always the result of intelligent effort."
-John Ruskin-

Not an Act, but a Habit—Mastery

If we were to look for two words that sum up how a Mensch lives his or her life it would be "mastery" and "grace." What's particularly remarkable about this is that this dual orientation permeates every aspect of a Mensch's life—whether personal or professional. It is reflected in a focused pursuit of quality through mastery. *Mastery* is a term that has received a lot of press and it is almost in danger of being trivialized. There are many definitions of mastery but, as George Leonard aptly observed, it resists true definition yet it can instantly be recognized. 'The Leader as a Mensch' is not defined by mastery, but by mastery of the self—that desire to surpass oneself, always striving to improve and rise above mere adequacy; whether in improving oneself or in the quality of one's relationships. This is not an easy undertaking, but for the Mensch, it is a path of joy; it is the only way to be.

What are the cornerstones of the pursuit of mastery and grace for 'The Leader as a Mensch'? It translates itself into two major areas: mastery of the self, and mastery of relationships. While mastery of one's profession is a given—and leaders devote years to perfect that aspect of their career—'The Leader as a Mensch' seeks another dimension. He or she knows that just as it is important to have financial acumen, industry knowledge and a global perspective, it is equally important to have the ability to attract the best talent, to foster open dialogue and to inspire trust. They know that just as it is crucial to have seasoned judgment, visionary thinking and strategic management, they also need to know how to build healthy organizational relationships, how to truly inspire others and leverage cultural diversity. They may have been taught to develop algorithms but 'The Leader as a Mensch' knows that developing people is also highly valuable.

The Mensch leader has a tremendous willingness to learn from everything and everyone. He or she seeks feedback and is not blindsided by unexplored weaknesses. This openness to others' input is a powerful tool in their self-development and is a clear indication of a graceful combination of humility and confidence at the same time. It is a fact that a person can be measured by the magnitude of what offends them—a Mensch has an emotional toughness and a self-assuredness that makes them impervious to what might derail others. They not only withstand criticism but seek it as a way to grow in their journey to being a quality leader. They might reject what their judgment tells them is subjective criticism, but they have the acumen and fortitude not to reject the person in the process. They are just too strong for that.

The end result of our work is a direct reflection of ourselves—'The Leader as a Mensch' believes that the quality of his or her relationships is also a reflection of himself or herself. He or she takes responsibility for the health of the relationship. Such leaders don't lose sight of the fact that forging bonds is the most crucial aspect of moving an organization forward. It is the quality of the relationships with everyone who is responsible for the work that is ultimately the factor that dictates the success or failure of any leadership effort. A Mensch knows that and spends as much care in developing rapport as he or she does in managing technology or developing strategic plans.

Mastery of the self involves staying calm in situations that have the potential to erode relationships. It entails being measured in one's response, considering the weight of a word that might land too heavily on someone and cause collateral damage. This is all a part of a composure that allows 'The Leader as a Mensch' to place the value of the relationship above the value of his or her ego. These leaders are capable of navigating any difficult situation without losing grace or control. We admire this form of mastery just as we admire the artist who plays the right chord without any dissonance.

This composure is part of executive presence, that elusive quality we all seek. What exactly is it? It's first and foremost something we notice in the quality of the communication—there is a candor; a directness of expression. Even though the communication is thought-ful, that is, the person has given some thought to what they will say and how they say it, there is an authentic ring to what is being said, an unmitigated honesty and clarity. The person with executive pres-ence is not closed minded and doesn't have a judgmental attitude. We see it in their eyes, in their demeanor, in their willingness to listen and be open to our ideas. They are solid in their self-assuredness, in the poise they exhibit while at the same time exuding warmth and showing an interest in us. They don't act impulsively and they listen more than they talk. All of these behaviors engage others and create an authentic connection. They are the framework that provides a stability and predictability in relationships even in times of flux and moments of difficulty. When we work with such a person, we can rely on the consistency in their behavior. It's like an unspoken pledge or promise to treat us well, a metaphorical surety against any damage to our sense of self.

How do we develop such a persona? How do we adopt this comportment and make it our own stamp of quality in all of our dealings? "Quality," said Aristotle, "is not an act, it is a habit." How can we incorporate these habits as part of our mission to be a true Mensch? First, we need to understand that the pursuit of mastery in any endeavor, while not easy, needs to be approached with a mindset of pleasure, not hardship. The expert on the subject of mastery is surely Dr. George Leonard. Let's take inspiration from the way he describes the journey. "How can I describe the kind of person who is on a path to mastery? First, I don't think it should be so dead serious. I think you should understand the joy of it, the fun of it." Seeing just how far you can go is a self-surpassing quality. Evolution is a story in mastery. "It's being real. It's being human. It's being who we are." The commitment to approach mastery of relationships needs to stem from a genuine desire for the greater good of others and our organizations; for our community and the world at large—not from a self-serving desire to be liked or admired. Without this nobility of purpose, without genuine intentions, our efforts are fruitless and perceived as hollow.

In the next pages, you will find some strategies for embarking on this most wonderful path—the path to master ourselves and our relationships and, in the process, develop the coveted quality we call executive presence. It goes beyond the surface aspects of having a polished appearance to having a polished heart. It is about incorporating grace in every human transaction. These strategies take a very short time to learn but your entire career to practice. As you live with grace in your life day after day, and as you watch the positive reactions engendered in your surroundings, you will come to the realization that grace in everything you do becomes a way of life; the way to achieve quality. The ultimate goal is not the medal, or the ribbon, but the path to mastery itself.

Leaves of Mastery

🕊 Grace is a sense of fitness and propriety. It is also a disposition to be generous and helpful. Think about your current relationships, whether direct reports, colleagues or superiors. Are you showing up with executive presence in all of them? Which relationships might need a tune-up or re-adjustment on your part? Is there someone you need to forgive for real or imaginary slights?

🕊 Every morning, spend a few minutes to visualize how you would like your day to evolve. In addition to the accomplishment of your 'to-do' list, think about how you can incorporate an attitude of good-will in all your dealings with everyone. In finance terms, goodwill is defined as an intangible asset representing the value of the company, such as its client base, its reputation and potential future earnings. It's the 'good name' of the business. Resolve to manage yourself with the same regard for your good name.

🕊 Create a relationship action plan. Make a chart of your key relationships at home and at work. How can you improve each relationship in the next six months?

🕊 When it comes to relationships, don't keep score. For more tips on becoming a master connector, consider reading *Never Eat Alone: And Other Secrets to Success, One Relationship at a Time* by

Keith Ferrazzi. We all know about the dreaded cold call. Consider the author's four tips for converting them to warm calls–conveying credibility, stating your value proposition, imparting urgency and convenience, and being prepared to offer a compromise.

❧ The relationship is the conversation. Know the difference between a conversation and a discussion. A discussion involves issues of right vs. wrong, it is an exchange of facts, opinions, and data. A conversation is a personal exploration of another person for the sole purpose of learning about them. To that end, read the insightful article written by Rabbi Noah Weinberg, "The 48 Ways to Wisdom."[27]

❧ Many of us inadvertently become 'conversation stealers', interjecting our own story to change the focus of the conversation to ourselves or to something we know. Should this be one of your habits, practice honoring the person's story before moving on to yours. Know when to speak and when to listen.[28]

❧ Make a point of remembering people's names and birthdays. It might seem like a small thing but it is a big thing in honoring others.

❧ Represent your unit or your company like an ambassador represents his or her country, conscious that everything he or she does and says casts a wide reflection. Practice dealing tactfully with others by making a decision to be diplomatic rather than aggressive. It is impossible to have true executive presence with an aggressive stance. This does not mean giving in, it means holding one's position with grace and regard for the other person. When criticizing others, it means replacing phrases such as "you need to" and "you must not…" with "I encourage you to…" or "you might consider how…". In addition, it involves replacing "don't…" and "you can't" with "it didn't work out well…" or "it seemed to me…".

❧ Focus on becoming a master communicator. Learn the art of storytelling and the value of the metaphor to inspire and influence others. There are many good books on this topic such as *The Leader's Voice* by Ron Crossland and Boyd Clark.

❧ Start collecting metaphors and symbols that you can use to hone your communication skills. (See Appendix for a comprehensive list of sources for metaphors.)

❧ Be conscious of being a good listener on the phone, not just in person.

❧ Do an audit of your emails and other virtual communication. Is your tone to your constituents cold and unintentionally abrupt? No matter how busy we are, we can warm up an email instantly by the addition of a person's name. If the matter is sensitive to the human side of the relationship, pick up the phone first. You can always follow up by email. We instinctively know this but take the shortcut because we are busy. This shortcut can become a burden in a relationship.

❧ Increasingly, younger constituents use Internet sites for communicating. Don't let yourself be out of touch with this important medium. At the very least, be informed about Facebook, Twitter, MySpace, LinkedIn, and Friendster.

❧ Executive presence is not being closed-minded. If you are not in the habit of doing so, carve out a little time to read one or two quality magazines to develop a broader view of the world and issues.

❧ Decide to do your own part to raise the level of the conversation—from things to ideas.

❧ Take a page from Eastern philosophies of management by considering practicing leadership *Aikido*. The term Aikido, roughly translates 'as the way of the harmonious spirit.' It refers to the non-combative martial art in Japan. In this imminently readable book, *Leadership Aikido: 6 Business Practices That Can Turn Your Life Around*, John O'Neil, President of The Center for Leadership Renewal, shows how individuals who practice leadership Aikido achieve an inner calm when under attack and can blend energy with a competitor to move forward. The three-pronged strategy of adaptability, flexibility and partnership is an unbeatable combination for personal mastery.

❧ What feedback mechanisms are in place in your organization? Are people encouraged to give feedback? If not, consider establishing a culture that values constructive criticism. One of the most thoughtful articles on providing and receiving feedback is Stephen M. Dent's *Feedback is Professional Development*. In it, he supplies *"The 3X Rule"* for feedback: "The first time I hear a piece of feedback; I thank the giver and tuck it away in my memory. The second time I hear the same piece of feedback from a different source, I listen a lot closer to what the person is saying. If I hear the same piece of feedback from a third party, I must decide if I am going to act on that feedback or not. This technique provides people with permission to not react immediately to feedback with a knee-jerk, defensive reaction, but gives them time to process the information they've received and determine for themselves its relevancy."[29]

❧ Being enlightened and judgmental at the same time is impossible. Choose enlightenment. This is admittedly one of the hardest things to do but it is also the most rewarding in our quest for relationship mastery. One way to practice being non-judgmental is to follow Walt Whitman's advice: practice being curious. Having the mindset of a relationship anthropologist changes the flavor of why people do what they do.

✒ Are you easily offended? Have you discarded some relationships because of a perceived offense? Landmark research by Dr. Raymond Bernard Cattell into personality dimensions describes people who score high on the trait of agreeableness as not easily offended. People who score high on this trait have a positive or optimistic view of human nature, believing that people are basically honest, decent and trustworthy. Consider that most people don't set out to purposely offend. Cultivate the trait of agreeableness by making a conscious effort not to take things personally. To that end, you might derive an inspiration from *The Four Agreements* by Don Miguel Ruiz and Don Jose Ruiz which espouses a powerful code of conduct based on the teachings of the ancient Toltec civilization. One of the four agreements is: Don't take anything personally. What others say and do is a reflection of their own reality.

✒ If you come across a class on executive presence, don't hesitate to enroll in it. It will pay dividends for your career.

Part Three

BRANCHES

Chapter Seven

*"An eye can threaten like a loaded and leveled gun, or it can insult
like hissing or kicking; or, in its altered mood, by beams of kindness,
it can make the heart dance for joy."*
-Ralph Waldo Emerson-

The Dimmer Switch of Performance—
A Leader's Mood

Mensches are individuals who smile with their eyes. They make
you feel safe. When they ask how you are—you have a sense that
they truly are interested in the answer. They have a presence when
they enter a room, that is, they command respectful attention, not
because of their title but because of their demeanor—you sense
someone who is at ease with who they are; very comfortable in their
own skin; self-assured without a shred of arrogance. They are totally
in the moment with you and they make you feel better about you.
They understand the huge impact that their moods can have on those
who work for them and they honor that responsibility by managing
their moods as carefully as they manage their duties as a leader. In fact,
they consider managing their moods one of the primary aspects of
leading with intelligence and heart. This is not an easy undertaking.

In response to a discussion on the effect of a leader's mood on the
performance of a team, a participant in a recent leadership workshop
made this heartfelt and realistic remark: "I cannot see how I am
expected to be in a good mood for four quarters in a row." The point
is well taken. But can you afford, as a leader, to even entertain this
thought? All of the research on employee performance points to the
contrary. There is a concept in French which is called *noblesse oblige*.

It implies that wealth, power, and prestige go hand-in-hand with certain social responsibilities—in other words, with privilege comes duty. It is a privilege when we have the opportunity to lead a team of people. However, with this privilege comes many responsibilities, chief of which, leadership pundits would contend, is managing moods.

In the *Harvard Business Review* article, "Leadership That Gets Results"[30], Dr. Daniel Goleman cites research which shows that up to 30 percent of a company's financial results (as measured by key business performance indicators such as revenue growth, return on sales, efficiency, and profitability) are determined by the climate of the organization.

So what is the major factor that drives the climate of an organization? It is the leader. In *Primal Leadership: Realizing the Power of Emotional Intelligence*, Dr. Goleman states that 50-70 percent of how employees perceive their organization's climate is attributable to the actions and behaviors of their leader. A leader creates the environment that determines people's moods at the office and their mood, in turn, affects their productivity and level of engagement.

Witness the number of times you may have driven home with an internal glow, reliving a positive encounter with an upbeat and supportive boss, perhaps savoring a *bon mot* about your performance that he or she left you with on a Friday afternoon—how great it made you feel, and how eager you were to get out of bed on the following Monday morning, and get back to the office to give that man or woman the very best that you had to offer. That's the afterglow that lingers and gives you renewed energy to be more productive, to bring your finest talents to work.

And think about the reverse of the afterglow—the aftermath, or bitter aftertaste. This is what Susan Scott in *Fierce Conversations: Achieving Success at Work and in Life, One Conversation at a Time*, brilliantly calls "The Emotional Wake." That's what lingers with you after being the recipient of some sharp or harsh remarks from a leader in a negative mood. How did that affect your determination to overcome difficulties in a project, to keep your heart fully engaged in the process, to want to continue to give that person your very best?

Leadership literature is full of studies attesting to the consequences of a leader's mood. One such study involved 62 chief executive officers and their top management teams; it showed that the more upbeat, energetic, and enthusiastic the executive team was, the more co-operatively they worked together, and the better the company's business results. The study also showed that the longer a company was managed by an executive team that didn't get along well, the poorer the company's market returns.

Perhaps nowhere is a leader's mood more crucial than in the service industry where employees in a bad mood can, without fail, adversely affect business. In one of a multitude of such studies involving 53 sales managers in retail outlets who led groups ranging in size from four to nine members, it was found that when managers themselves were in an upbeat, positive mood, their moods spilled over to their staff, positively affecting the staff's performance and increasing sales. We can all take an inspiration from organizations such as Whole Foods who place great value on the importance of creating a positive climate for employees which, in turn, ensures a pleasant customer experience and repeat visits. One of their values is: Supporting team member happiness and excellence. Their website includes the following statement: "Our success is dependent upon the collective energy and intelligence of all of our team members. We strive to create a work environment where motivated team members can flourish and succeed to their highest potential. We appreciate effort and reward results."

When we move the curtain a bit, we can see clearly that a leader's bad mood is a source of infection; an emotional contagion that eventually spreads across people to entire units. We can learn a thing or two from leadership in the military. Imagine the effect on troop morale and energy that an overwhelmed, anxious, worried or irate leader would have? And how about a leader who is plagued by uncertainty? "Indecision," as H.A. Hopf says, "is contagious. It transmits itself to others." It can become debilitating and habit-forming in an organization, as people take their cues from the leader's state of mind.

We could argue that the occasional bad mood, the occasional rant, on a bad 'corporate hair day,' is excusable. Often, we refer to this type of behavior with statements such as, "she can't control her temper sometimes, but she is so brilliant." Or we say, "he has an amazing mind but he has a tendency to shout at people when it's stressful." It is as though brilliance is an excuse for bad behavior. And it may very well be in some environments—but the message it sends to constituents is one of inconsistency, which is an undesirable trait in any leader. We want our leaders to be predictable because there is comfort and safety in predictability. Predictability engenders trust and an unpredictable leader elicits anxiety and, in some cases, even fear—both of which negatively affect performance and productivity.

Of course, no leader steps out of the elevator in the morning with an intention to spread a bad mood around but, as sure as there is gravity, events occur during the course of some days that can derail even the best among us. To be clear, we are not advocating that leaders turn into a shrink wrapped version, complete with false smiles and fake cheerfulness. Constituents spot a non-genuine smile anyway and are very adept at noticing when a leader infantilizes them.

There are, of course, no easy solutions to managing emotions on an hourly basis in the often difficult circumstances in which leaders must operate and make decisions. However, we can draw some advice from another *Harvard Business Review* article by Dr. Daniel Goleman et al. entitled, "Primal Leadership: The Hidden Driver of Great Performance."[31] First of all, it's important to note that a leader's mood has the greatest impact on performance when it is upbeat. But it must also be in tune with those around him. Goleman et al. refer to this as Dynamic Resonance. "Good moods galvanize good performance, but it doesn't make sense for a leader to be as chipper as a blue jay at dawn if sales are tanking or the business is going under. The most effective executives display moods and behaviors that match the situation at hand, with a healthy dose of optimism mixed in. They respect how other people are feeling—even if it is glum or defeated—but they also model what it looks like to move forward with hope and humor." This is the way of 'The Leader as a Mensch.' The operative three words here are: optimism, hope, and humor. As someone once put it, leaders are dealers in hope. An example of a leader who understood this is Charles M. Schwab who said, "I consider my ability to arouse enthusiasm among men the greatest asset I possess, and the way to develop the best that is in a man is by appreciation and encouragement."[32]

If you cringe at the whole notion of emotions in the workplace; talk of empathy, compassion and intuition; or discussions focused on emotional intelligence, I encourage you to reconsider this mindset. Hone your intuitive ability, and listen to those hunches that hint to you that something in your behavior and actions on bad days is causing a ripple effect on others. These are the whispers we try to dismiss when we elect to focus only on rationality. Intuition is a precious tool worth including in our kit. Albert Einstein put it best: "The intuitive mind is a sacred gift and the rational mind is a faithful servant. We have created a society that honors the servant and has forgotten the gift."

Part of your responsibility as a leader is to create a good place for people to deliver their best work. It is difficult for people to excel at doing something they don't enjoy. Do people enjoy working for you? Check some of the strategies at the end of this chapter for minimizing your role in creating potential employee stress.

As the leader, you have in your hand the switch that can control the intensity of engagement of the people who do the work in your organization. It's like being a director in a movie. "The first work of the director is to set a mood so that the actor's work can take place." (William Friedkin, American movie and television director/producer.) A leader's upbeat mood metaphorically oxygenates the blood of followers—it's a transfusion into the corporate arteries. It may be one of the most potent contributions you can make as a leader. It's being a Mensch.

Leaves of High Performance

🐦 Take a hard look at your behavior in meetings, which are often 'cauldrons of emotion.' Do you model the way by setting a positive tone right from the start? Or do you impose your own pace based on how you feel at the moment? Aim for a calm, relaxed mood, and a consistent, positive approach.

🐦 Look for good in others. Long before leadership books were in vogue, André Malraux, French novelist and statesman, reminded us that one of the central objectives of a leader is to make others aware of the greatness that lies in them. Be known in your organization as someone who is always on the lookout for what is right with people. It engenders good will and is good for business.

🐦 Read the climate. Do you have a good reading of the climate of your unit or organization? Can you accurately sense what the emotional atmosphere is? Is it upbeat? Is it energized? Is it down or dejected? Do people seem slightly apprehensive and somewhat cautious in your presence? Can you ask a trusted acolyte if the atmosphere changes when you are away?

🐦 Be pleasant and cooperative. If you are an emergent leader, and working on having a pleasant personality is not a priority for you, consider putting some effort into cultivating this prized quality. It is almost impossible to have executive presence without it. Be cooperative, for example sharing ideas and shortcuts. This is another example of how mood affects productivity.

❦ Be emotionally attractive. This links to the concept of resonant leadership. Resonant leaders are individuals who have the ability to manage their own emotions and those of others in a manner that drives the success of their teams and organizations. *In Resonant Leadership: Renewing Yourself and Connecting with Others through Mindfulness, Hope and Compassion*, Richard Boyatzis and Annie McKee explain that resonant leaders create a positive emotional tone in the organization and engage and inspire people. As the title of their book indicates, these leaders possess three core qualities: mindfulness, hope, and compassion. Consider making these a part of your arsenal as a leader.

❦ Manage the emotions of change. Be particularly mindful of how you manage emotions if your organization is undergoing change: how you handle emotions during these crucial times can help or hinder the change process. It's a known fact that if the resistance to change is emotional, it is the hardest form of resistance to overcome. As the leader handling a change initiative, don't avoid the emotions that accompany the change process. Set the mood and manage the emotions—or they will manage you.

❦ Promote responsibly. Consider the notion of the seldom-talked-about unwelcome promotion. While everyone can be trained to be a leader, the truth is, not everyone enjoys leading. Some individuals targeted for a management promotion may be too reluctant to voice their apprehension for fear of making a less than favorable impression. They accept the promotion and function poorly under stress. This in turn creates difficulties for all those who are subjected to the reluctant leader. If you are responsible for others, resolve to consider this when handing out promotions. Make it 'safe' for talented individuals to march to the beat of a different drum. You can derive an inspiration from 3M Company, a firm which provides their technical people with parallel dual career paths called the Dual Ladder System. This means that individuals can still progress in their careers in terms of compensation and other manifestations of advancement without having to enter the management ranks. For example, this approach honors those who excel without forcing them to stray from their natural R&D habitat.

Give your people a head start. Making sure that your newly-minted leaders have the appropriate tools needed for their people management responsibilities is a key requirement to helping them succeed and minimizing the stress. This includes mentoring, providing a relevant leadership skills assessment to uncover strengths and areas for development, assisting in the creation of a learning action plan and providing leadership training and/or coaching. It also means providing ongoing support and feedback. Sadly, some of these initiatives are sometimes rushed in as an emergency measure after the rookie leader has caused some casualties. Often, these interventions, because they are brought in after the fact and in response to problems, are perceived by the new leader as a criticism and as remedial action which may be embarked upon reluctantly. Providing these tools and services before, or just at the start of the promotion, on the other hand, is seen as a perk and a sign of the company's investment in the individual's career development.

Create flow. Knowing that the skills we have are adequate for the job is one of the requirements for being 'in the flow', that marvelous state of consciousness described by Mihály Csíkszentmihályi,

PhD, Professor of Psychology and Management at the Drucker and Ito Graduate School of Management at Claremont Graduate University. In his book, *Flow: The Psychology of Optimal Experience*, Csíkszentmihályi explains 'flow,' or being in the zone, as a state of consciousness where we are so absorbed by what we are doing that we don't even notice the passage of time—hours feel like minutes. I liken it to those times when we are so enthralled in a project or a task, so engaged, that we forget to eat. For flow to occur, we need to have a balance between our skills and the high challenges we are tasked with. When the challenge is high, yet the skill set for the challenge is low, we are in a state of anxiety. If this condition persists for prolonged periods of time, without relief, we enter a cycle of stress which could lead to burn out. Do you know where your team members are in terms of flow? How can you create flow for each of them? Are you setting and communicating crystal clear goals and expectations, not only for the long-term but more importantly for the short-term? This is one of the conditions for creating flow. Do you provide immediate feedback on how well a person is performing— helping that person understand the effect of his or her efforts? While every job has routine, non-challenging aspects, you need to be aware of where your constituents are in terms of job challenge vs. skill set and making an effort, wherever possible, to design jobs that take full advantage of your constituents' talents and to continually raise the bar.[33]

Help your people develop stress-hardy personalities by focusing on three Cs: Commitment, (being committed to something that is meaningful, i.e., work, community, family; staying engaged and involved in ongoing events, even in the most trying of circumstances, rather than feeling isolated); Control (believing in their ability, through their efforts, to turn events to their advantage rather than adopting a passive and powerless victim mode) and Challenge (viewing change, whether positive or negative, as an opportunity to learn rather than as a threat).

❧ Create a Stop Doing List. Borrowed from Jim Collins' *Good to Great: Why Some Companies Make the Leap... and Others Don't*, creating a Stop Doing List is useful in minimizing stress and achieving clarity of focus. Those who built companies that went from 'good to great' "... displayed a remarkable discipline to unplug all sorts of extraneous junk". We all have To Do Lists but how many of us have created a list to isolate and halt pursuits that don't serve us well any longer? Can you benefit from creating a Stop Doing List? What are your energy drainers? Are these among some of the offenders that may cause you stress: internalizing others' criticism, fragmented boundaries, power struggles, unprotected personal time, useless networking, continuous one-way favors? What can you do to address these and other drainers so that you can stay in your power and reduce your stress? What can you eliminate to make room for what energizes you and brings you closer to achieving your goals?

❧ Focus on what you do best. If business strategy is a cause of stress, consider reading this focused, well-researched and insightful book, *Profit From the Core: Growth Strategy in an Era of Turbulence* by Chris Zook and James Allen. It reaffirms the timeless tenet that focusing on your core business—that which you do best—is the most efficient way to bring about long-term growth and profit. By refocusing on what you do best, the authors advise, it will also be easier to spot inefficiencies that drain your business. The book contains many actionable ideas and shows how to identify your company's core business and define your competitive advantage in order to be able to discover and evaluate opportunities for expanding into related businesses—what Zook refers to as Logical Adjacencies. Among the multitude of practical, well-reasoned ideas contained in this book is also a list of key management questions for evaluating adjacencies. The concept transcends business—if we don't narrow down our activities to a fundamental core from which we can grow, a strategy becomes much harder to develop.

☙ Know what is not worth fighting for: Pick your battles wisely. How often have we heard this? Yet, in the heat of the moment, do we stop for a second and think "Is this truly worth fighting for? Are you even likely to win?" An example of such a no-win battle which can easily occur in the workplace is fighting the power behind the throne. That is, entering into a contest of wills with a person who has no apparent authority but who has great influence. This individual is very adept at working behind the scenes and you can easily find yourself unwittingly on thin ice, wasting your valuable, non-renewable energy. Long ago I came across a statement: "Maturity is being content to know that you are right without having to prove someone else wrong." How much stress we could eliminate if we were guided by such a philosophy? What if we decided to devote each day only to that which is worthy of our attention—our personal achievements and our organization's achievements?

☙ Shorten your meetings: If lengthy non-productive meetings are among the stressors, consider learning and introducing to your team a tool such as Edward de Bono's Six Thinking Hats™. It's a long-standing, proven and useful tool for parallel thinking that encourages cooperation, reduces conflicts, and helps run more focused, efficient meetings. Briefly, the technique entails separating thinking into six important functions, each one of which is identified with a colored symbolic thinking hat that represents a different style of thinking.

The six styles of thinking or perspectives are: white hat for facts, figures and data; black hat for judgments, cautions, downsides and risks; yellow hat for positive views and benefits; green hat for creativity, alternatives, solutions; red hat for gut feel, intuitions and emotions; blue hat for overview, process control, organizing and action items. Individuals can easily orchestrate an agenda for the meeting that lays out a sequence of hats or thinking. By mentally and concurrently wearing and 'switching the same colored hats', individuals can focus and redirect thoughts and the conversation, as appropriate. (For more information, go to http://www.edwdebono.com.)

~❧ Focus on what matters: Minimizing stress also means looking at our life through a holistic lens—addressing our needs in each area, whether it is physical, emotional, intellectual, psychological, or social. What are some daily practices that you can introduce to create reserves in each of these important areas of your life? Reserves help us when we feel depleted from the day's stressors. If you need inspiration in this area, consider reading Dr. John C. Maxwell, *Today Matters: 12 Daily Practices to Guarantee Tomorrow's Success*. Maxwell provides 12 practical guidelines such as practicing and developing good thinking to gain an advantage, practicing commitment to gain tenacity, pursuing growth to give us potential and developing priorities to give us focus. Regarding priorities, is reading and responding to pointless emails the first thing you do when you start the day? What about reversing the order? Focusing first on projects that will give you the highest returns for yourself and your organization? Imagine the benefits of establishing this simple initiative as a daily practice. The book is a reminder that we choose our life by how we spend time. People who achieve their potential act on their priorities every day.

~❧ Know how you spend your time: Along the same lines, one of the most useful tools I came across for stress management is Stephen Covey's Time Management Matrix in his 1995 book entitled *First Things First: To Live, to Love, to Learn, to Leave a Legacy*. The matrix involves creating four quadrants: Urgent/Important; Not Urgent/Important; Urgent/Not Important; Not Urgent/Not Important. After using the matrix to do a forensic analysis of how you spend your time, take remedial steps to focus on what 'really' matters in your life. Ask yourself: "What is one activity, if done superbly well and consistently, would have significant positive results in my personal life?" Then ask the same questions regarding your professional life.

Become a master at synthesizing information: A catch-all phrase for multitasking, continuous technology interruptions and the information overload that we are bombarded with daily is "cognitive overload."[34] Leaders are particularly vulnerable to cognitive overload as they are typically required to consider a lot more information than the rest of us. Interestingly, in an article by Dr. Howard Gardner, "The Synthesizing Leader," which appeared in The *Harvard Business Review List: Breakthrough Ideas for 2006* (February 1, 2006), we learn that the single most important trait of future leaders in the developed world is the ability to synthesize information… to decide what information to heed, what to ignore, and how to organize and communicate that which we judge to be important."[35] Synthesizing which information to consider entails, among other things, developing standards for selection, such as source credibility and relevance. We must ask questions such as "Does this information form a coherent story? "Do these trends make sense?" In our data rich world, selecting which pieces of information are worthy of our ever shrinking attention span, is a key competency for reducing stress and, ultimately, being more effective as a leader.

Chapter 8

"The true meaning of life is to plant trees,
under whose shade you do not expect to sit."
-Nelson Henderson-

Degrees of Giving—Generosity

I am holding in my hand a graceful inspirational book entitled *Ramban's Ladder: A Meditation on Generosity and Why It is Necessary to Give* by Julie Salamon. The book is based on the teachings of Ramban, a physician and philosopher who, more than a thousand years ago, developed Ramban's Ladder which outlines the various forms of giving—from the lowest (handing money begrudgingly, as one might to a panhandler) to the highest (helping someone become self-reliant). I have long been meditating on the whole issue of *generosity* as an important quality of leadership, observing leaders who had it and those who lacked it.

When we think of generosity, thoughts automatically drift to gifts of money or charity. While this is important in the context of leadership, there are other gifts that don't have a monetary value but whose value is beyond price. These include giving someone a chance, giving someone the benefit of the doubt and giving others a reason to want to work for you. It entails giving others latitude, permission to make mistakes and all the information that they need to do the job. It means giving them the authority that goes with responsibility—giving them due credit for their ideas. In a nutshell, all of this translates to generosity of spirit, a quality we admire in leaders.

Generosity, a word whose etymology means of noble birth, used to be associated with members of the aristocracy who, by virtue of their privileges, were expected to show generosity towards those in lesser standing. Leaders too, by virtue of their position, and the power and privileges that they hold relative to those they lead, have the same expectations and obligations. A prime obligation is to lead with a generous heart, to be guided by a nobility of mind. A leader's generosity has a positive spreading effect—conversely its absence, has a series of negative consequences that, if a leader paused to reflect on them, might stop him in his tracks.

I am a firm believer that people need more than just a nice job close to home. Most people want to find meaning in their jobs—they want to feel that they are a part of something bigger and something better. They want to know that what they do matters. A leader with a generous spirit understands this need and connects the dots for people—the dots that help them see how the work they perform, no matter how small it may be in the scheme of things, has a bearing on the ultimate vision of the company. There is a well-known anecdote that is related by Tom Peters about a hospital in the US that treats cancer. During a series of staff interviews, an interviewer asked the housekeeper what her job entailed. She responded, "I help to cure cancer." Somewhere in that hospital, a leader connected the dots for this individual and made her feel that she was an integral part of the hospital's mission. Do you do that for the people who do the work in your unit or organization? There is a lot of talk these days about lack of engagement in the workforce. Imagine how engaged people are when their leader makes them feel that they are a fundamental part of the success of the organization, that everyone, from the receptionist or mail clerk to the vice president of product development, constitutes a binding thread, tightly interwoven into the company fabric—each equally doing its part to give the fabric its strength.

A leader who incorporates the many facets of generosity of spirit is like the multifaceted diamond which gives the highest possible light. Take for example something as simple as the gift of laughter. We have all witnessed how the higher someone is in the organization, the funnier we tend to find their anecdotes and humor. How about the obverse? Think of a time when someone junior said something humorous in a meeting but, in our harried schedule to move on with the agenda, we may not take a few seconds to acknowledge the person or his or her humor. Inadvertently, we subtly rob people when we do that and we may never know the tiny repercussions in terms of loss of confidence. When a leader takes a moment to give others the gift of laughter, he gives them a gift that says you, too, are important to this team.

A leader with a generous spirit delegates not just routine work but understands about delegating 'worthwhile' work that becomes a gift of development and growth for someone else. How we love those leaders! These are the leaders that make us want to get out of bed in the morning and go to work to give that person the very best that we have to offer. These are the leaders who get our discretionary effort, every day.

And what about gifts of information? In a survey on effective motivation published by 1000 Ventures, one of the top items that individuals want in the workplace is the ability to be "in" on things. This was rated 9 on a scale of 1 to 10, with 10 being the highest. Managers ranked this item as 1. This is a large gap in a leader's understanding of his or her constituents. The quickest way to satisfy this need in constituents is to share information. We have all come across some leaders who are inclined to hoard crucial information as the currency of power. Leaders with a generous spirit give employees a chance to get under the hood and to be a part of the inner circle. Freely and generously sharing know-how, expertise, and ideas is not only beneficial for employees—it's a smart way of doing business. Similar to the 'boundaryless organization' concept of Jack Welch, former Chairman and Chief Executive Officer, General Electric (GE), a chief executive officer I worked for at one time had this as his mantra: "All support, no walls." Sharing of information was one of the keys to his ethos. Leaders at the top need to model this aspect of generosity as a strategic imperative. Think, for example, how damaging it is to have a culture of secrecy where everyone hoards information and expertise vital to the business. Not only does it harm innovation, but it can literally cripple departments as individuals quit and take their knowledge out the door with them. We never know the true cost of this until it is too late, if ever. A study on emotional intelligence found that software developers with high EQ (Emotional Quotient) developed software three times as fast as those with low EQ. The reason? Those with high EQ shared shortcuts. Making people feel like owners instead of hired hands ensures that we get their minds and hearts as well as their hands.

Albert Camus said, "Real generosity toward the future consists in giving all to what is present." How often, as leaders, are we so focused on future achievements, on realizing the vision of the organization, that in the process, we neglect who is there. A leader of a successful software firm confessed to me once that she woke up one day realizing how much she had disconnected emotionally from the people who did the work in her organization while focusing on the strategic imperatives of the company. Today, we have a tendency to be too soaked in self-absorption. We become excessively self-involved to the point where, without intending it, we exclude others and we often only consciously take notice that we have excluded them when they have become disengaged. Self-absorption inherently prevents generosity.

There is an African village that uses the expression, "I am here if you are here" for the greetings of "good morning" and "hello." Imagine the gift we give others when we are fully present with them—when we truly see them. Perhaps this is what Ralph Waldo Emerson meant when he said, "The only gift is the gift of thyself." Bill Clinton recently ended a speech to a 6,000-member audience with an exhortation to "see more people." This preceded his reference to all the people who do the clean-up work behind the scenes after the audience leaves. Do we give a thought to the people who are unnoticed in our organizations, those who quietly work in the background?

It is difficult to write about generosity without reflecting on Friedrich Nietzsche's thoughts on generosity as being a core virtue, a central aspect of his ethics. What is of particular importance is his notion that generosity is "abundance in oneself... affirmation of one-self." Practicing generosity is about self-value and about being generous to one-self. What gifts can you give yourself, on a daily basis, which would enhance your persona as a leader, as a person in the community or as a friend? Unconditional self-acceptance leads to accepting others. We cannot appreciate others if we don't appreciate ourselves. We cannot have empathy for others if we don't have empathy for ourselves. And that requires the discipline of leadership. Nietzsche says it best, "If one is not firm and brave with oneself, one has nothing to bestow and cannot stretch out one's hand to protect and support."

While generosity in its pure sense is altruistic, there is still a reciprocity to generosity, the surprise dividends in the form of a recycling of good will, a surplus of cooperation and the sheer satisfaction of seeing another benefit from our giving of ourselves—our time, our attention, our knowledge, the very best that we have to offer to those who cross our paths at work or life. We will never know what opportunities we may have missed in life by showing up tight-fisted. It is hard to receive anything if we don't open our hands to give.

This anonymous finding struck a chord in me. Perhaps it might in you too. "If you're a generous person, you'll have no trouble admitting that somebody else is good. If you're a better person, you'll find it's a total impossibility." It crossed my mind that, ironically, the author of this quote may have intentionally wanted to remain anonymous. There is grace in giving without wanting to be identified as the donor. This is *Ramban's 7th Degree of Giving*. As a leader, giving people the gift of not just our appreciation for their good work, but our genuine admiration of their talents, is generosity of spirit at its pinnacle. This is the difference in saying to someone "Great job." versus "This was pure genius!". It is also the difference in saying to someone "I appreciated your help." versus "I couldn't have done it without you!" When it comes to genuine praise, like the sun at high noon, give resplendently. When you see good work, say it and say it from the heart, just as you thought it. Free up the thought and let it breathe. Let it fly out there in the form of generous words and watch what you get back. Giving is ultimately sharing.

Leaves of Generosity

Here are some practical tips to enhance our generosity of spirit:

🍂 In Adele Lynn's book, *In Search of Honor: Lessons from Workers in How to Build Trust*, we learn that 55 percent of workers value giving people a sense of importance as the number one item for building trust in the workplace. Consider what small actions you could take today to intentionally make people feel that the work they do is important and that they themselves, as people, are important to your team.

🍂 If giving frequent criticism is your style of management, consider some of these questions: Is your motivation genuine or is it to gain points? Are you picking the right moment? Are you stopping to reflect how you might deliver the criticism while still honoring the other person? For example, is the criticism causing you to view the person with contaminated lenses, as a problem to be fixed, rather than a gifted person that you want to inspire to greater achievements? Are you comparing the person to someone else? Even with our best intentions, this is likely to cause unnecessary resentment.

🍂 Giving people visibility in your organization is a special gift we bestow to help others shine and grow. I encourage you to think how you might give people more access to senior executives, more access to your boss. Consider as well that people like to know that their boss's boss knows the great contributions they made to a project or the significant effort in writing a report that does not bear their name. Knowing that a leader is representing them well to upper management is a high octane motivator, and engenders fierce loyalty. It's great potency for you. The more we do this, the more we strengthen our own power and self-confidence as leaders.

☙ Real generosity of spirit is doing something for someone without their knowledge. Think of one or two deserving persons in your organization that you can help by planting a career enhancing seed on their behalf—perhaps saying something positive about their work to someone in authority?

☙ The Reverend Martin Luther King, Jr. said: "The old law of an eye for an eye leaves everyone blind." Consider how harboring vindictive thoughts, even though so compelling at times, is nothing but violence to oneself. A characteristic of a generous person is a total lack of resentment—it's in effect, being too noble, too big for that. Who do you need to forgive? What do you need to let go of?

☙ Consider doing an audit of how you spend your time. How much of it is spent on self-actualization activities and how much is spent on focusing outward? Do you need to re-balance this focus?

☙ There is a saying that "charity begins at home but shouldn't stay there." What small or big acts can you do to show charity at the office, both materially and spiritually?

☙ Look around you and pick someone who needs encouragement and resolve to give them that. Consider that some people have never received encouragement in their life—not from teachers, not from bosses, not even from parents. In this regard, watch this inspiring video clip by Steve Sjogren on being an 'Inside-Out Leader' on http://nz.youtube.com/watch?v=T2XDBbHwAWw.

☙ One of the most valuable gifts we can give someone is giving them a chance. Is there someone right now to whom you could give a second chance to prove themselves? If so, what active steps can you take to create the right circumstances for them to succeed? What doors can you open for someone who is well-deserving but not well positioned to be noticed?

❧ Practice *"The 80/20 Rule"* in communication: Listen 80 percent of the time and talk for 20 percent of the time. Watch how others respond when this happens. No one ever complains of being listened to too much.

❧ Is there someone on your team who has a habit of appropriating others' ideas and repeating them as though they are their own? Be vigilant for this behavior and subtly correct the individual by saying something like, "That's a good idea. Jillian brought this up earlier. Let's discuss it." It is your responsibility as a Mensch leader to protect your people from the bad behavior of others in any team meetings that you run.

❧ Consider adding the reflective listening technique as part of your ongoing gifts as a leader. Reflective listening, an identifying mark of a generous spirit, requires focus and very active participation. It includes: (1) Paraphrasing what you heard in question form (Statement: "He shouldn't have done that." Response: "You feel that there were better strategies he could have followed?"); (2) Giving visual encouragement to the person to continue talking (giving them full eye contact, nodding… the repertoire of the classic good listener); (3) Listening for the emotions behind the statement (Statement: "I can't work late another evening." Response: "You sound frustrated."). Generally, people have a subconscious desire for their emotions to be acknowledged and recognized. Reflective listening is a bridge to our relationships and a skill well worth spending the effort to master.

❧ Resolve to become a philanthropist of know-how. What

knowledge, expertise or best practices can you share with others as a way to enrich them? For inspiration, read about other leaders who practice teaching in their organization for everyone's benefit— for example, Jack Welch used to fill his calendar with hundreds of personal hours teaching managers and executives at the company's training center in Croton-on-Hudson, New York; and Andy Grove, ex-Chief Executive Officer of Intel, devoted an equal amount of time to personally teaching new hires and senior managers his philosophy on how to lead in an industry where innovation goes stale very quickly.

☙ Public speaking is known to be amongst the greatest fears experienced by millions of people. The next time you attend a presentation given by an apprehensive team member, practice giving them moral support. The simplest of generous acts can be to abstain from checking your Blackberry, giving the odd nod in agreement, and practicing looking with kind eyes.

☙ If you are a male leader, consider that the women in your group may not have equal opportunities to meet with you and the other team members on a social level if a large number of the social events surround sports activities, such as golf. This gives the men an extra advantage in forming strong bonds. As a caring and thoughtful leader, be aware of this disparity and resolve to remedy it.

☙ Give others a reason to want to work for you. If your direct reports were asked to list 20 reasons why they would want to work for you besides earning a living, what would these reasons be? Would this list make you proud of yourself as a leader? If not, what can you do today to start changing this?

☙ Is there someone on your team who disappointed you? Does this person deserve a second chance? If the answer is yes, don't wait until it is too late.

☙ We never get a second chance at making first impressions. Go against this precept by allowing someone, who failed to impress you at first, show you different sides of himself or herself. Sometimes people blow their first encounter with us by trying too hard and therefore acting in a manner that does not reflect their best side.

☙ Take some inspiration from Walt Whitman's beautiful words, "The habit of giving enhances the desire to give." It's like building a muscle. It requires practice and persistence—once it becomes habitual, you will emerge as a stronger leader.

Chapter Nine

"Appreciation is like looking through a wide-angle lens that lets you see the entire forest, not just the one tree limb you walked up on."
-Doc Childre-

The Biggest Hunger—Appreciation

Lao-tzu, the Father of Taoism said, "To see things in the seed, that is genius." This is what we now refer to as Appreciative Intelligence,[36] a term coined by Dr. Tojo Thatchenkery, to describe the capacity by certain individuals to see the positive inherent generative potential of situations or people. It is the ability to see a breakthrough product, top talent, or valuable solution of the future that is not readily visible in the present situation. In short, it is the ability to see "the mighty oak in the acorn." The term originated when Thatchenkery began studying the explosive entrepreneurial growth in Silicon Valley in the late 1990s. According to the author, it is appreciative intelligence that allowed, partly, for so many highly talented immigrants from different countries to assemble in the area and flourish. As the author puts it, venture capitalists looking to fund the right ideas were asking the question "How can I make this work?" as opposed to "What are the chances this idea will fail?" They created an environment of high anticipation of positive results which became a contagious fever of opportunity, achievement, resilience and possibility recognition.

Appreciative Intelligence is different from Appreciative Inquiry which is an approach and methodology for analyzing organizations. Appreciative Intelligence is a mental ability of individuals who have a knack for reframing situations (the glass half full/half empty), and a keen eye for spotting what's valuable and positive in a situation or in people. And these individuals go one step further: they are able to envision how the positive aspects can be used to create a better future. 'The Leader as a Mensch' is a happy combination of the two, i.e., he or she is a leader with Appreciative Intelligence using an Appreciative Inquiry approach. This is what makes such a leader a powerful force indeed for effecting positive change and inspiring others to give the very best they have to offer. Imagine if all leaders in an organization proactively and mindfully practiced appreciative intelligence. Imagine the profound, healthy impact that this would have on an organization's culture.

Such a culture would fuel employees' motivation. Surveys of what employees want consistently rank 'appreciation for work well done' high on the motivation index—well above 'good wages.' Ironically, managers often place good wages above *appreciation* in their responses of what employees want.

Other surveys show that one of the reasons employees leave companies is because of lack of praise and recognition. Leaders often talk of the challenge of building trust in their organization. Adele B. Lynn's study on trust in the workplace[37] shows that 54 percent of those polled would work for less remuneration if the following trust-building factors were present: (1) Importance: giving people a sense of importance about who they are and about their role in the organization; (2) Touch: feeling that the leader genuinely cares about them, feeling a connection with the leader; (3) Gratitude: being appreciated for their contributions and sacrifices; receiving genuine gratitude; (4) Fairness: knowing that leaders ensure equal and fair distribution of rewards.

These trust-building qualities are what a Mensch learns at his or her mother's knee, a way of being that is strengthened and deepened with the passage of years—and one that we can all adopt in our journey to be a Mensch for those we lead. They are deeply engrained ways of doing business that engender enormous trust in the work-place. They are the oasis in the desert, the place where "Menschhood" becomes power.

Mensches understand the fundamental truths about people, they know, at a cellular level, that recognition and praise are indeed high octane fuel for the soul. When we receive a genuine compliment, we experience an inner glow—a warm, magical feeling that makes us break into a smile. It makes us want to go the extra mile for the person who bestowed the sincere compliment. If this were not important to us, we would not be treasuring all of the mementos of awards, plaques, appreciative notes, emails and other tokens of appreciation that we receive over the years.

Intuitively, of course, we all know that genuine appreciation is a key factor in our relationship with our constituents and any Management 101 course will touch on the value of praising employees for their contributions. Yet, many well meaning and otherwise caring leaders are reluctant to express their appreciation of others' gifts and contributions.

Many years ago, I worked for a caring leader, one who genuinely appreciated his constituents. He confided in me one day that he found expressing praise a very difficult thing to do publicly; even harder to do privately. I asked him why and he said, "I grew up in a household where praising each other was not something we did." There is a profound implication in this statement. Our families are our first corporations—that's where we learned many of our behaviors and it is often difficult to break these ingrained patterns. Withholding praise, however, is a pattern of behavior that we need to unlearn if we want to bring the best out in people. We need to get over the embarrassment that grips some of us when we have to praise an individual. Perhaps the ultimate appreciation is letting people know that their work, no matter how far they are from the top of the pyramid, is important to the organization. It's about making everyone feel like an owner and helping them understand how their work contributes to the overall purpose of the company. It's about practicing "seeing more people." Excellence involves everyone. There is another lovely Chinese quote that says, "A bit of perfume always clings to the hand that gives roses." As leaders, when we make people feel great about themselves, paradoxically, we elevate ourselves to greatness as well.

In a recent CNN Interview, Arun Sarin, Chief Executive Officer, Vodafone, the world's leading mobile telecommunications company, states, "The power of the leadership role in some ways is to encourage others in an organization to shine and for them to do great things." Sarin gets personally involved where he feels that he can make a difference in encouraging others to bring their very best to work. He represents a leader with high self-awareness who strongly believes in modeling himself in terms of what he expects from others. He reflects not only on whether he is doing the right things strategically or from an operational execution standpoint, but also from the standpoint of leading the team properly from a human point of view: "Am I encouraging people, am I communicating, am I giving them enough room?"[38]

A fundamental quality of 'The Leader as a Mensch' is the appreciation of others—seeing others not as a problem to be fixed but as a reservoir of skills, talents and ideas to be nurtured and developed. But just as we cannot provide care in an emergency until we have first cared for ourselves, I encourage you to apply the dynamic concept of Appreciative Intelligence on yourself. Practicing appreciating our own talents and our gifts opens us up to appreciating others' greatness.

I am afraid of spiders. On a cognitive level, I know that they are harmless little creatures. But if I see a spider web in my basement, I am immediately on the alert for the dangerous intruder. And when I spot one of them, I experience cortical inhibition. Because of this mild phobia, the word "spider" catches my attention whenever I see it in print. Such was the situation when, during the course of unrelated research, I learned that, if we have a fear of spiders, we are more likely to notice them. This is exactly what happens in my household. I am always the one who discovers the lone spider in the basement while others are oblivious to its peaceful existence.

If we are anxious about something, we are more likely to notice what we perceive as a threat than those who are relaxed. In other words, whatever we focus on, we see. This is a powerful concept with significant implications for both our personal and organizational lives. What we see is deeply influenced by what we expect. Over the years, many scholars have worked on variations of this concept, such as The Rosenthal Effect, also known as the Pygmalion Effect[39] (a psychological finding where a leader's high expectations of others causes high performance) and the obverse, the Set Up To Fail Syndrome[40] (where low expectations causes low performance). While these concepts have to do with expectations we have of others, the Galatea Effect[41] (named after the stone statue of the beautiful woman that the sculptor Pygmalion brought to life) is about expectations individuals have of themselves—it occurs, in effect, when high self-expectations become the catalyst for greater personal achievements. When this happens, we become our own 'positive self-fulfilling prophecy'—a significant factor in employee performance. 'The Leader as a Mensch' sets out to help employees believe in themselves, in their ability to perform well, and sets the stage for their possibility to succeed. The confidence that results from employees' high personal expectations in turn spurs them to higher achievement and productivity. Their performance rises to the level of their own expectations.

Perhaps the scholar who has done the most work in this area is Stanford University's Dr. Albert Bandura who pioneered the concept of Self-efficacy.[42] Self-efficacy is our belief in our ability to perform effectively. Bandura's theory is that individuals who have high self-efficacy expectations (those who believe that they can achieve what they set out to do), are healthier, more effective, and generally more successful than those with low self-efficacy expectations.

High self-efficacy determines many of the choices we make; the higher our self-efficacy, the more likely we are to seek new challenges and persist in the face of adversity or failure. High self-efficacy also influences the effort that we put into achievements. One might say that we are what we think we are.

This old adage is now scientifically proven. From the extensive brain research that is being conducted, we know that our brains are not hard wired. We know that the brain is plastic, and has the ability to reorganize itself every time we have new experiences. According to Dr. John Kounios, Drexel University Medical School Professor of Psychology and Cognitive Neuroscience, our neural connections change even after a 20-minute conversation![43] This gives new meaning to the positive impact that a conversation can have with a coach or mentor when it focuses on high expectations that we have of ourselves. It also showcases the advantage and good fortune we have when we happen to work for a Mensch leader.

What are your thoughts about yourself, about your untapped potential? On a scale of 1 to 10, how would you rate your self-efficacy? What expectations do you have of yourself? What do you want to attract in your professional and personal life? What do you want to be known for in your leadership? I have posed these questions to a dozen or so highly successful professionals in the technical arena that I have had the good fortune of interacting with in the last six months. Without fail, everyone mentioned high expectations about their future and the majority being at a mid-life point, is looking for deeper philosophical answers to the profound question: "what's next for me?" in planning the future.

One individual in the group I questioned directed me to a book that had a particular impact on him entitled *Creating the Good Life: Applying Aristotle's Wisdom to Find Meaning and Happiness.*[44] Authored by James O'Toole, (Research Professor, Center for Effective Organizations at the University of Southern California, and Mortimer J. Adler, Senior Fellow at the Aspen Institute), the book takes us through the author's own search for a better life and explores, among other things, how one resolves tensions between family and work commitments, how we find meaning and fulfillment, and how we create a good society within our own firm, even if we only have one person reporting to us. "If Aristotle is right that the good life depends on developing one's human potential, then providing the conditions in which employees can do so is a clear moral responsibility of leaders of work organizations… [Leaders who] deny employees the chance to develop their potential deny them the opportunity to develop their humanity."

This insightful study prompts one to do some serious self-exploration on issues such as:

- What does it mean to lead a good life?
- To be happy, what should I be doing that I am not doing now? And what am I doing now that I should stop doing?
- How can I create the opportunity of happiness for the people who work for me?
- How should I begin to develop self-discipline so that I can focus on what will make me happy in the long term?

- What is personal excellence and how do I achieve it?
- How can I be a success in my specialized career, and, at the same time, a well-rounded person with a wide range of interests and knowledge?
- To what extent does my personal happiness entail a relationship with the community of others?

To live one's life to its full potential, in accordance to the Aristotelian precepts, requires emotional and intellectual self-rigor. It also requires the ability to have high expectations of oneself, expectations that one might succeed at what appears to be a lofty vision. If the possibility of generating creative and fulfilling experiences that fill our hearts and minds does not seem real and feasible, then we need to question the underlying assumptions that get us to see what we see and dispute those assumptions; acting as our own defense lawyer.

What are the higher steps you need to climb to unlock your full potential on your 'Leader as a Mensch' journey? What are the 'buts' that you need to eliminate from your vocabulary in order to break through to new levels of personal achievement? What mindsets might you need to change to stay ahead of the curve? Charles M. Schwab put it aptly: "None of us is born with a stop-valve on his powers or with a set limit to his capacities. There's no limit possible to the expansion of each one of us." As for me, I need to stop seeing spiders as objects of fear and stop to marvel, instead, at the wondrous creativity of their intricate silk webs.

Practice seeing others, truly seeing them in their utmost potential and remind yourself, every day, of the power of appreciation. It will help you create a culture where people are willing to share their ideas and insights for the success of your organization. Mother Teresa said, "There is more hunger in the world for love and appreciation than for bread." This applies to everyone, at every level, in every corner of the world.

Leaves of Appreciation

🌿 If you have difficulty praising others, analyze the root causes of this. If it is a fear of embarrassing others, know that even the most introverted individuals who shun public praise, enjoy reading an email to all staff about their contributions. If it is discomfort at not knowing how to do it, read the few simple rules below and consider working with a coach for one or two sessions on this most important aspect of a leader's communication repertoire. Self-awareness precedes self-management.

🌿 Sometimes, withholding praise is simply due to a lack of time for leaders who are required to handle an ever-increasing number of issues during the course of a harried day. If this is your challenge, I encourage you to reframe how you view this particular issue. Showing your people that you care about their needs should move up on your To Do list. It takes less than 10 seconds to say: "I appreciate the time and thought you put into this report. It is exceptional. Thank you."

🌿 Praise has a limited "best before" date. Don't delay its expression or wait until performance review time—when you see something that is worthy of praising, do so promptly after the event.

🌿 Make your genuine words memorable for your constituents by being specific about the achievement. Not many of us remember the perfunctory "job well done" but we all remember someone who tells us "This was pure genius!" or "I would have missed this if you hadn't picked it up." Praise does not have to be elaborate. It just needs to be genuine.

✒ When you drop by an employee's office or cubicle to deliver the praise, don't follow your praise with a conversation about business matters or other projects. Deliver the praise and leave. Come back later for discussions on other matters. This gives the praise its moment of honor and heightens its value in the eyes of the recipient.

✒ A primer for rewarding and recognizing others is Jim Kouzes' and Barry Posner's *Encouraging the Heart: A Leader's Guide to Rewarding and Recognizing Others.* The book provides 150 ways to encourage the heart. Another useful book is Steven Kerr's, *Ultimate Rewards: What Really Motivates People to Achieve.* The book outlines many different sources of motivation including accountability, responsibility, organizational culture, coaching, teamwork, incentives, and goal setting.

✒ If you are the head of a department attending a staff event celebrating an employee's contributions, be totally present in the moment. Don't check your watch, take phone calls or otherwise be preoccupied. As the leader, people notice all of your actions and micro-expressions. If business imperatives prevent you from being fully present, it is best to let the employee's immediate supervisor attend the celebration—you can drop into the employee's office later, when you are free, to personally congratulate the employee. I am reminded once again of that African greeting "I am here if you are here." Practice being fully present for these celebrations.

✒ Think about the people who report to you or the people you influence during the course of your work. What can you do to help them lift their vision to higher sights? What can you do to help them reframe their self-limiting beliefs?

❧ Understand *"The Magic Ratio of 5 to 1"*. Daniel Kahneman, Nobel Prize-winning scientist, discovered that we experience approximately 20,000 individual moments in a working day. Each moment lasts a few seconds. The memorable moments are almost always positive or negative, rarely the neutral ones. Think about the frequency of positive to negative interactions in your team. Is the balance tipped in favor of the positive? In the course of research involving married couples, John Gottman, psychologist, discovered that successful marriages have a 5 to 1 ratio of positive to negative interactions. The same applies to the workplace. Consider increasing your self-awareness in this area. For tips on how to increase your magic ratio, read *How Full is Your Bucket: Positive Strategies for Work and Life* by Tom Rath and Donald O. Clifton.[45]

❧ Compliment a direct report in front of other people. It's a gift and a welcome boost to anyone's day.

❧ Practice self-appreciation. It is the foundation for self-confidence and inner stability without which you will be anxious and tense in your leadership journey. If this is lacking in your life right now, make it a priority. Work with a coach, if necessary, to help you focus on what you do well and what you can do even better. Spend time with confident people. If you make mistakes, seriously reflect on what happened and extract the learning. Consider the value of music in positively impacting your emotions. To that end, start collecting upbeat music that you can listen to before an important meeting or presentation.

❧ Encourage others to appreciate themselves. Be conscious about creating opportunities at work for others to appreciate themselves. For example, give direct reports a chance to shine at meetings; make space for them to be heard in a group setting; encourage their ideas by modeling the way for others; give them choice assignments that carry prestige; create opportunities for them to have visibility in the company; represent them well to upper management; send them to conferences on your behalf. You will be fulfilling one of the noble goals of leadership which is to help others become leaders themselves.

◦❧ Remember the stories that others tell you about themselves. When people relate a story about their life experiences, ambitions, dreams, and challenges, they give us a part of themselves. Typically people become more animated and enthusiastic when they speak of themselves. Honor that emotional investment on their part by making an effort to remember their stories.

Epilogue

Thomas Carlyle said, "The best effect of any book is that it excites the reader to self-activity." It is my sincere wish that this book has opened up for you a wide portal that leads to the road traveled by 'The Leader as a Mensch'. If you are already a Mensch leader, congratulate yourself. You don't need this book. Perhaps you can gift it to someone who can benefit from it. If you are a leader who knows in his heart that being a Mensch on a consistent basis is a difficult undertaking, I congratulate you for reading this book. Resolve to pick up one 'leaf' at a time and use it until 'it' becomes who you are, every day. Being a Mensch leader is, at times, a difficult path but one that will ultimately be richly rewarding for you as you witness how it can improve your corner of the world, and make a positive difference in the lives of those you lead. I wish you the best in achieving your recognition as a Mensch Leader. To contact me, please write bmartinuzzi@increaseyoureq.com.

Appendix A

Mensch Library

Humility

Jim Collins, "Level 5 Leadership: The Triumph of Humility and Fierce Resolve," *Harvard Business Review*, 01 July 2005 *Downloadable pdf.*

Jim Collins, *Good to Great: Why Some Companies Make the Leap... and Others Don't.* (New York: Random House, 2001).

David Marcum and Steven Smith, *Egonomics: What Makes Ego Our Greatest Asset (or Most Expensive Liability).* (New York: Fireside, 2007).

Joseph L. Badaracco Jr., *Leading Quietly: An Unorthodox Guide to Doing the Right Thing.* (Boston: Harvard Business School Press, 2002).

Authenticity

Bill George, *Authentic Leadership: Rediscovering the Secrets to Creating Lasting Value.* (San Francisco: Jossey-Bass Pfeiffer, 2003).

Bill George, Peter Sims, *True North: Discover Your Authentic Leadership.* (San Francisco: Jossey-Bass, 2007).

Terry Pearce, *Leading Out Loud: Inspiring Change through Authentic Communication.* (San Francisco: Jossey-Bass Wiley, 2003).

Kevin Cashman and Jack Forem, *Awakening the Leader Within: A Journey to Authenticity and Purpose.* (Hoboken: John Wiley & Sons Inc., 2003).

Daniel Goleman with Warren Bennis, *The Power of Truth: A Leading with Emotional Intelligence Conversation with Warren Bennis.* Audio Book. (New York: Macmillan Audio, 2006).

Empathy

Richard E. Boyatzis and Annie McKee, *Resonant Leadership: Renewing Yourself and Connecting with Others Through Mindfulness, Hope, and Compassion.* (Boston: Harvard Business School Press, 2005).

J.B. Kellett, R.H. Humphrey, and R.G. Sleeth, "Empathy and the Emergence of Task and Relations Leaders," *The Leadership Quarterly,* Volume 17, Issue 2, April 2006.

Daniel H. Pink, *A Whole New Mind: Moving from the Information Age to the Conceptual Age.* (New York: Riverhead Hardcover, 2005).

Arbinger Institute, *Leadership and Self Deception: Getting Out of the Box.* (San Francisco: Berrett-Koehler Publishers, 2002).

John Selby, *Listening with Empathy: Creating Genuine Connections with Customers and Colleagues.* (Charlottesville: Hampton Roads Publishing Company, Inc., 2007).

Accountability

Patrick M. Lencioni, T*he Five Dysfunctions of a Team: A Leadership Fable.* (San Francisco: Jossey-Bass, 2002).

Brian Dive, *The Accountable Leader: Developing Effective Leadership through Managerial Accountability.* (London: Kogan Page Limited, 2008).

Max DePree, *Leadership is an Art.* (New York: Currency/Doubleday, Random House, Inc., 2004).

Optimism

Dr. Martin E. P. Seligman., *Learned Optimism: How to Change your Life and Your Mind.* (New York: Free Press, 1998).

Dennis N. T. Perkins et al., *Leading at the Edge: Leadership Lessons from the Extraordinary Saga of Shackleton's Antarctic Expedition.* (New York: AMACOM, 2000).

Price Pritchett, *Hard Optimism.* (New York: McGraw-Hill, 2006).

Mastery

Belle Linda Halpern and Kathy Lubar, *Leadership Presence.* (New York: Gotham Books, 2004).

Tony Dungy and Nathan Whitaker, *Quiet Strength: The Principles, Practices, & Priorities of a Winning Life.* (Carol Stream: Tyndale House Publishers, 2007).

Boyd Clarke and Ron Crossland, *The Leader's Voice.* (New York: The Tom Peters Press and SelectBooks Inc., 2002).

Marshall Goldsmith with Mark Reiter, *What Got You Here Won't Get You There: How Successful People Become Even More Successful.* (New York: Hyperion, 2007).

Howard Gardner, *Five Minds for the Future.* (Boston: Harvard Business School Press, 2006).

Richard Strozzi-Heckler and Richard Leider, *The Leadership Dojo: Build Your Foundation as an Exemplary Leader*. (Berkeley: Frog Books, 2007).

Carol Keers and Thomas Mungavan, *Seeing Yourself as Others Do: Authentic Executive Presence at Any Stage of Your Career*. (Wayzata: Significant Pursuit Publishing, 2008).

Moods

Daniel Goleman, Richard Boyatzis, and Annie McKee, *Primal Leadership*. (Boston: Harvard Business School Publishing, 2002).

Tom Rath and Donald O. Clifton *How Full is Your Bucket: Positive Strategies for Work and Life*. (New York: Gallup Press, 2004).

Joshua Freedman, "White Paper: Emotional Contagion," http://www.6seconds.org.

Joshua Freedman, "Organizational Vital Signs," http://www.6seconds.org/tools/ovs.php.

Generosity

James M. Kouzes and Barry Z. Posner, *Encourage the Heart*. (San Francisco: Jossey-Bass, 2006).

Ken Blanchard and S. Truett Cathy, *The Generosity Factor: Discover the Joy of Giving Your Time, Talent, and Treasure*. (Grand Rapids: Zondervan, 2002).

Donna Deeprose, *How to Recognize and Reward Employees: 150 Ways to Inspire Peak Performance*. (New York: AMACOM, 2006).

Appreciative Intelligence

Tojo Thatchenkery and Carol Metzker, *Appreciative Intelligence: Seeing the Mighty Oak in the Acorn*. (San Francisco: Berrett-Koehler Publishers, 2006).

Steven Kerr, *Ultimate Rewards: What Really Motivates People to Achieve*. (Boston: Harvard Business School Press, 1997).

Tom Rath and Donald O. Clifton, *How Full is Your Bucket: Positive Strategies for Work and Life*. (New York: Gallup Press, 2004).

Mike Robbins, *Focus on the Good Stuff: The Power of Appreciation*. (San Francisco: Jossey-Bass, 2007).

John C. Maxwell and Les Parrott, *25 Ways to Win with People: How to Make Others Feel Like a Million Bucks*. (Nashville: Thomas Nelson, 2005).

Michael Ray, *The Highest Goal: The Secret That Sustains You in Every Moment.* (San Francisco: Berrett-Koehler Publishers, 2004).

Gregg Thompson and Susanne Biro, *Unleashed! Expecting Greatness and Other Secrets of Coaching for Exceptional Performance.* (New York: Select Books, Incorporated, 2007).

The Taxonomy of Leadership

James MacGregor Burns, *Leadership.* (New York: Harper & Row, 1979).

James M. Kouzes and Barry Z. Posner, *The Leadership Challenge.* (San Francisco: Jossey-Bass, 2003).

Kevin Eikenberry, *Remarkable Leadership: Unleashing Your Leadership Potential One Skill at a Time.* (San Francisco: Jossey-Bass, 2007).

Warren Bennis, *On Becoming a Leader.* Cambridge: Perseus Book Group, 2003).

Joshua Freedman, *At the Heart of Leadership. How to Get Results with Emotional Intelligence.* (San Francisco: Six Seconds Emotional Intelligence Press, 2007).

Daniel Goleman, "Leadership That Gets Results", *Harvard Business Review,* Mar 1, 2000.

Daniel Goleman, "What Makes a Leader", (HBR Classic) *Harvard Business Review,* January 2004.

Edward E. Morler, *The Leadership Integrity Challenge: Assessing and Facilitating Emotional Maturity.* (Sonoma: Sanai Publishing, 2006).

Marcus Buckingham and Curt Coffman, *First Break All the Rules: What The World's Greatest Managers Do Differently.* (New York: Simon & Schuster, 1999).

Susan H. Gebelein, Kristie J. Nelson-Neuhaus, Carol J. Skube, David G. Lee, Lisa A. Stevens, Lowell W. Hellervik, and Brian L. Davis (Editors). *Successful Manager's Handbook.* (Minneapolis: ePredix, 2004).

Susan H. Gebelein, David G. Lee, Kristie J. Nelson-Neuhaus, Elaine B. Sloan, *Successful Executive's Handbook.* (Minneapolis: Personnel Decisions International, 2004).

Reuven Bar-On, R. Handley, and S. Fund, T*he Impact of Emotional and Social Intelligence on Performance.* (2006), in Vanessa Druskat, Fabio Sala, and Gerald Mount (Eds.), *Linking Emotional Intelligence and Performance At Work: Current research evidence.* (Mahwah, NJ: Lawrence

Erlbaum), 3-19.

Reuven Bar-On, J. G. Maree, and M. J. Elias, (Eds.), *Educating People to be Emotionally Intelligent*. (Westport, CT: Praeger, 2006).

Reuven Bar-On, and J. D. A Parker, J.D.A., *Handbook of Emotional Intelligence: Theory, Development, Assessment and Application at Home, School and in the Workplace*. (San Francisco: Jossey-Bass, 2000).

General

William F. Baker and Michael O'Malley, *Leading with Kindness: How Good People Consistently Get Superior Results*. (New York: AMACOM, 2008).

James M. Kouzes (Editor), Barry Z. Posner (Editor), *Christian Reflections on The Leadership Challenge*. (San Francisco: John Wiley & Sons, 2004).

Dalai Lama—Ethical Leadership Video, "The Dalai Lama discusses ethical leadership for a new millennium to promote dialogue and cross-cultural understanding around the world." http://www.learnoutloud.com/Free-Audio-Video/Religion-and-Spirituality/Religious-Figures/His-Holiness--The-XIV-Dalai-Lama/19407.

Metaphor Sources

James Rowe Adams, *From Literal to Literary: The Essential Reference Book for Biblical Metaphors*. (Bend: Rising Star Press, 2005).

Scott Chou (Author), David Brower (Editor), *Maxims, Morals, and Metaphors: A Primer on Venture Capital*. (Salt Lake City: Aardvark Global Publishing Company, 2008).

Dr. Mardy Grothe, *I Never Metaphor I Didn't Like: A Comprehensive Compilation of History's Greatest Analogies, Metaphors, and Similes*. (New York: HarperCollins, 2008).

George Lakoff and Mark Johnson, *Metaphors We Live By*. (Chicago: University of Chicago Press, 1980).

Metaphor Sites from UMBC, http://userpages.umbc.edu/~lharris/metalist.htm.

Appendix B

Inspirations

"For man is a tree of the field."
-Deuteronomy 20:19-

The Human Tree

Based on the teachings of the Lubavitcher Rebbe.

"Man is a tree of the field," and the Jewish calendar reserves one day each year—the New Year for Trees on the 15th of Shevat—for us to contemplate our affinity with our botanical analogue and what it can teach us about our own lives.

The tree's primary components are: the *roots*, which anchor it to the ground and supply it with water and other nutrients; the *trunk*, *branches* and *leaves* which comprise its body; and the fruit, which contains the seeds by which the tree reproduces itself.

The spiritual life of man also includes roots, a body, and fruit. The roots represent faith, our source of nurture and perseverance. The trunk, branches and leaves are the body of our spiritual lives—our intellectual, emotional and practical achievements. The fruit is our power of spiritual procreation—the power to influence others, to plant a seed in a fellow human being and see it sprout, grow and bear fruit.

ROOTS AND BODY

The roots are the least glamorous of the tree's parts, and the most crucial. Buried underground, virtually invisible, they possess neither the majesty of the tree's body, the colorfulness of its leaves nor the tastiness of its fruit. But without roots, a tree cannot survive.

Furthermore, the roots must keep pace with the body: if the trunk and leaves of a tree grow and spread without a proportional increase in its roots, the tree will collapse under its own weight. On the other hand, a profusion of roots makes for a healthier, stronger tree, even if it has a meager trunk and few branches, leaves and fruit. And if the roots are sound, the tree will rejuvenate itself if its body is damaged or its branches cut off.

Faith is the least glamorous of our spiritual faculties. Characterized by a simple conviction and commitment to one's Source, it lacks the sophistication of the intellect, the vivid color of the emotions, or the sense of satisfaction that comes from deed. And faith is buried underground, its true extent concealed from others and even from ourselves.

Yet our faith, our supra-rational commitment to God, is the foundation of our entire tree. From it stems the trunk of our understanding, from which branch out our feelings, motivations and deeds. And while the body of the tree also provides some of its spiritual nurture, the bulk of our spiritual sustenance derives from its roots, from our faith in and commitment to our Creator.

A soul might grow a majestic trunk, numerous and wide-spreading branches, beautiful leaves and lush fruit. But these must be equaled, indeed surpassed, by its roots. Above the surface, there might be much wisdom, profundity of feeling, abundant experience, copious achievement and many disciples; but if these are not grounded and vitalized by an even greater faith and commitment, it is a tree without foundation, a tree doomed to collapse under its own weight.

On the other hand, a life might be blessed with only sparse knowledge, meager feeling and experience, scant achievement and little fruit. But if its roots are extensive and deep, it is a healthy tree: a tree fully in possession of what it does have; a tree with the capacity to recover from the setbacks of life; a tree with the potential to eventually grow and develop into a loftier, more beautiful and fruitful tree.

FRUIT AND SEED

The tree desires to reproduce, to spread its seeds far and wide so that they take root in diverse and distant places. But the tree's reach is limited to the extent of its own branches. It must therefore seek out other, more mobile couriers to transport its seeds.

So the tree produces fruit, in which its seeds are enveloped by tasty, colorful, sweet-smelling fibers and juices. The seeds themselves would not rouse the interest of animals and men; but with their attractive packaging, they have no shortage of customers who, after consuming the external fruit, deposit the seeds in those diverse and distant places where the tree wants to plant its seeds.

When we communicate with others, we employ many devices to make our message attractive. We buttress it with intellectual sophistication, steep it in emotional sauce, dress it in colorful words and images. But we should bear in mind that this is only the packaging—the fruit that contains the seed. The seed itself is essentially tasteless—the only way that we can truly impact others is by conveying our own simple faith in what we are telling them, our own simple commitment to what we are espousing.

If the seed is there, our message will take root in their minds and hearts, and our own vision will be grafted into theirs. But if there is no seed, there will be no progeny to our effort, however tasty our fruit might be.

Source: http://www.MeaningfulLife.com
http://www.chabad.org/library/article_cdo/aid/2775/jewish/The-Human-Tree.htm

How to Be a Mensch

A blog entry from Guy Kawasaki, MBA
Co-founder of Alltop.com, and author of *Reality Check*.

I have a theory (as opposed to a dream) that Heaven is a three-class Boeing 777. You can sit in a narrow seat that doesn't recline and eat chicken-like substances next to a screaming baby in coach class. Or, you can sit in a slightly wider seat that reclines slightly more and eat a beef-like substance in business class.

But the goal is to spend eternity in first class; specifically Singapore Airlines first class. Here your seat reclines to a completely flat position, and there's a power outlet, personal video player, wireless access to the Internet , and noise-cancelling headphones. There are also chefs, not microwave ovens.

You cannot buy your way into first class; nor can you use frequent flyer miles. The only way to earn an upgrade is to be a Mensch. Leo Rosten, the Yiddish maven and author of *The Joys of Yiddish*, defines Mensch this way:

Someone to admire and emulate, someone of noble character. The key to being "a real Mensch" is nothing less than character, rectitude, dignity, a sense of what is right, responsible, decorous.

Here is my humble attempt to help you achieve Menschdom.

1. *Help people who cannot help you.* A Mensch helps people who cannot ever return the favor. He doesn't care if the recipient is rich, famous, or powerful. This doesn't mean that you shouldn't help rich, famous, or powerful people (indeed, they may need the most help), but you shouldn't help only rich, famous, and powerful people.

2. *Help without the expectation of return.* A Mensch helps people without the expectation of return—at least in this life. What's

the payoff? Not that there has to be a payoff, but the payoff is the pure satisfaction of helping others. Nothing more, nothing less.

3. *Help many people.* Menschdom is a numbers game: you should help many people, so you don't hide your generosity under a bushel. (Of course, not even a Mensch can help everyone. To try to do so would mean failing to help anyone.)

4. *Do the right thing the right way.* A Mensch always does the right thing the right way. She would never cop an attitude like, "We're not as bad as Enron." There is a bright, clear line between right and wrong, and a Mensch never crosses that line.

5. *Pay back society.* A Mensch realizes that he's blessed. For example, entrepreneurs are blessed with vision and passion plus the ability to recruit, raise money, and change the world. These blessings come with the obligation to pay back society. The baseline is that we owe something to society—we're not a doing a favor by paying back society.

Exercise: It's the end of your life. What three things do you want people to remember you for?

1.

2.

3.

If you'd like to read more about this subject, I suggest Joshua Halberstam's book entitled *Everyday Ethics: Inspired Solutions to Real-Life Dilemmas.*

Source: Guy Kawasaki, MBA
http://blog.guykawasaki.com/2006/02/how_to_be_a_men.html

Appendix C

Emotional Intelligence Frameworks for Becoming a Mensch

The Six Seconds' EQ Model

Six Seconds is a global not-for-profit organization helping people create a positive future by using the power of emotional intelligence. The Six Seconds Model provides an action plan, a process framework, for tapping the power of EQ. It starts with three pursuits: "Know Yourself," "Choose Yourself," and "Give Yourself."

1. *Know Yourself*—awareness. Increasing self-awareness, recognizing patterns and feelings, lets you understand what "makes you tick" and is the first step to growth.

2. *Choose Yourself*—intentionality. Building self-management and self-direction allows you to consciously direct your thoughts, feelings, and actions (vs reacting unconsciously).

3. *Give Yourself*—purpose. Aligning your daily choices with your larger sense of purpose unlocks your full power and potential. It comes from using empathy and principled decision making to increase wisdom.

Within these three pursuits are eight core competencies that are measurable and learnable. They are:

Know Yourself	Choose Yourself	Give Yourself
Enhance Emotional Literacy	Apply Consequential Thinking	Increase Empathy
Recognize Patterns	Navigate Emotions Engage Intrinsic Motivation Exercise Optimism	Pursue Noble Goals

Each of the eight competencies in this model is essential for putting emotional intelligence into action. Each competency has value to you as a leader—and as a person. Taken together they will help you influence others, build full commitment, make great decisions, and lead and live to your highest intentions.

Source: http://www.6seconds.org

The Bar-On Model of Emotional Intelligence

Dr. Reuven Bar-On developed one of the most widely used measures of emotional intelligence, the "EQi." The EQi is a measure of socially and emotionally effective function, and measures the array of competencies and traits in the Bar-On model. There are five key areas and sub-scales under each.

INTRAPERSONAL
(Self-Awareness and Self-Expression)

- Self-Regard
  (Being aware of, understanding and accepting ourselves)
- Emotional Self-Awareness
  (Being aware of and understanding our emotions)
- Assertiveness
  (Expressing our feelings and ourselves nondestructively)
- Independence
  (Being self-reliant and free of emotional dependency on others)
- Self-Actualization
  (Setting and achieving goals to actualize our potential)

INTERPERSONAL
(Social Awareness and Interaction)

- Empathy
  (Being aware of and understanding how others feel)
- Social Responsibility
  (Identifying with and feeling part of our social groups)
- Interpersonal Relationship
  (Establishing mutually satisfying relationships)

STRESS MANAGEMENT
(Emotional Management and Control)

- Stress Tolerance
  (Effectively and constructively managing our emotions)
- Impulse Control
  (Effectively and constructively controlling our emotions)

ADAPTABILITY
(Change Management)

- Reality Testing
  (Validating our feelings and thinking with external reality)
- Flexibility
  (Coping with and adapting to change in our daily life)
- Problem Solving
  (Generating effective solutions to problems of an intrapersonal and interpersonal nature)

GENERAL MOOD
(Self-Motivation)

- Optimism
  (Having a positive outlook and looking at the brighter side of life)
- Happiness
  (Feeling content with ourselves, others and life in general)

Source: http://www.reuvenbaron.org

The Emotional Competencies (Goleman) Model

The Emotional Intelligence (EI) model introduced by Dr. Daniel Goleman proposes Emotional Intelligence as a mixture of competencies and skills that drive leadership performance. There are four areas:

Self-Awareness concerns knowing one's internal states, preferences, resources, and intuitions. The self-awareness cluster contains three competencies:

- Emotional Awareness
  (Recognizing one's emotions and their effects)
- Accurate Self-Assessment
  (Knowing one's strengths and limits)
- Self-Confidence
  (A strong sense of one's self-worth and capabilities)

Self-Management refers to managing one's internal states, impulses, and resources. The Self-Management cluster contains six competencies:

- Emotional Self-Control
  (Keeping disruptive emotions and impulses in check)
- Transparency
  (Maintaining integrity, acting congruently with one's values
- Adaptability
  (Flexibility in handling change)
- Achievement
  (Striving to improve or meeting a standard of excellence
- Initiative
  (Readiness to act on opportunities)
- Optimism
  (Persistence in pursuing goals despite obstacles and setbacks)

Social Awareness refers to how people handle relationships and awareness of others' feelings, needs, and concerns. The social awareness cluster contains three competencies:

- Empathy
  (Sensing others' feelings and perspectives, and taking an active interest in their concerns)
- Organizational Awareness
  (Reading a group's emotional currents and power relationships)
- Service Orientation
  (Anticipating, recognizing, and meeting customers' needs)

Relationship Management concerns the skill or adeptness at inducing desirable responses in others. The relationship management cluster contains six competencies:

- Developing Others
  (Sensing others' development needs and bolstering their abilities)
- Inspirational Leadership
  (Inspiring and guiding individuals and groups)
- Change Catalyst
  (Initiating or managing change)
- Influence
  (Wielding effective tactics for persuasion)
- Conflict Management
  (Negotiating and resolving disagreements)
- Teamwork & Collaboration
  (Working with others toward shared goals. Creating group synergy in pursuing collective goals.)

Source: http://www.eiconsortium.org

Appendix D

Final Words

Things to Consider On Your Path to Becoming a Mensch

- Avoiding negative environments.
- Continuing to learn throughout your lifetime—reading books, attending courses, acquiring new skills, upgrading yourself.
- Using your time wisely. It's a non-renewable resource.
- Unraveling what may hold you back.
- Consistently acting with integrity—even in small things.
- Knowing that no one else can identify our paths for us. Listen to your inner voice and follow its guidance.
- Working hard to achieve what you want—study those who achieved success: very few did it without hard work.
- After making a mistake, analyzing what happened so that you don't repeat it. "People are only a victim the first time. After that, they are a volunteer."
- Improving your presentation skills. It will pay dividends for your career.
- When someone has wronged you, continuing to treat them with civility—it's a Mensch thing to do.
- Becoming conscious of your self-talk.
- Becoming aware of your "hot buttons"—those events that can rob you of your grace.
- Making sense of your life's journey—don't leave it to chance.
- Putting energy and care into all of your communications.
- Bringing grace into all of your relationships.

- Giving way more than you take.
- Hiring people who are as smart as you, or smarter.
- Considering your flaws from the vantage point of your strengths: almost always, your strengths outnumber your flaws.
- Finding an area that you can excel in and throwing yourself into it wholeheartedly.
- Knowing that your example is more important than your advice.
- Listening—it's one of the most powerful tools for connecting with others.
- Consider how others feel when they are in your presence. Do they feel better about themselves? This will say a lot about you.
- Cultivating your network as you would a precious asset. Relationships require integrity and on-going maintenance in order to thrive. Don't tap into your network only when you need them.
- Understanding that emotions are contagious.
- Helping a child develop a positive self-image—it will be your greatest gift.

Endnotes

1. See also Jim Collins, "Level 5 Leadership: The Triumph of Humility and Fierce Resolve," *Harvard Business Review OnPoint Enhanced Edition*, 01 January, 2001.

2. Prem Benimadhu, *"Pat Daniel—Authentic Voice," The Conference Board of Canada's Leaders on Leadership Series*. July, 2003.

3. Mark W. Merrill of *Indianapolis Star* on Anthony Kevin "Tony" Dungy, http://www.coachdungy.com/saying.asp.

4. "TIME's 100 Most Influential People in the World," http://www.underthenews. blogspot.com/2007/05/times-100-most-influential-people-no.html.

5. Edward Frederick Halifax, British Statesman (1881-1959).

6. Bill George, *Leadership: Rediscovering the Secrets to Creating Lasting Value*. (Hoboken: Wiley, John & Sons, Inc., 2004), 12.

7. Mike Leibling and Robin Prior, *Coaching Made Easy: Step-by-Step Techniques That Get Results*. (Philadelphia: Kogan Page Publishers, 2004), 15.

8. Joseph Campbell, *The Power of Myth*. (New York: Knopf Publishing Group, 1991), 186.

9. Elisa Birnbaum, "Leadership in Focus: Monica Patten," http://www.charityville.com/cv/archive/alead07/alead0701.html, 02 January, 2007.

10. Daniel Goleman with Warren Bennis, *The Power of Truth: A Leading with Emotional Intelligence Conversation with Warren Bennis*, DVD. (New York: Macmillan Audio, 2006).

11. Steve Rubel, *The Art of Listening*. http://www.micropersuasion.com/2004/11/the_art_of_list.html.

12. James Park, *Becoming More Authentic: The Positive Side of Existentialism*. (Minneapolis: Existential Books, 2007), 36.

13. Ron Crossland, *The Leader's Voice*. (New York: The Tom Peters Press and SelectBooks, Inc., 2002), 128.

14. Dr. Antonio Damasio, *Descartes' Error: Emotion, Reason, and the Human Brain*. (New York: Putnam Publishing, 1994).

15. Some of these studies can be viewed on the website of The Consortium for Research on Emotional Intelligence in Organizations, http://www.eiconsortium.org.

16. Carrie Ann Wharton, http://www.cognitive-psychology.suite101.com/article.cfm/mirror_neurons.

17. "Mary Robinson Biography," http://www.knowledgerush.com.
18. Emma Reilly, "Maple Leaf President Michael McCain Proves Mettle," Canadian Press, 01 September, 2008.
19. Tom Peters, "Tom Peters Blog Archives–September 2004," http://www.tompeters.com.
20. http://www.goalpro.com
21. Bass, B. M. and Avolio, B. J. (1993). "Transformational Leadership: A Response to Critiques;" M. M. Chemers and R. Ayman (Eds.), *Leadership Theory and Research: Perspectives and Directions* (San Diego: Academic Press, 1993) 56.
22. Dr. Martin E. P. Seligman, 1990.
23. Bachman et al., cited by Cary Cherniss.
24. Lorenzo Fariselli, Massimiliano Ghini, and Joshua Freedman, "Optimism and Job Performance," http://www.6seconds.org/sei/research.php/2006.
25. Lorraine Segil, "What Makes a Dynamic Leader? Energy: Opportunistic Optimism," http://www.womensmedia.com/new/segil-leader-optimism.shtml.
26. Dr. Martin E. P. Seligman, *Authentic Happiness: Using the New Positive Psychology to Realize Your Potential for Lasting Fulfillment.* (New York: The Free Press, 2002).
27. http://www.aish.com/ The_Art_of_Conversation.asp
28. http://www.matilijapress.com
29. http://www.leader-values.com
30. "Leadership That Gets Results," *Harvard Business Review*, 01 March, 2000.
31. "Primal Leadership: The Hidden Driver of Great Performance," *Harvard Business Review,* 01 December, 2001.
32. Charles M. Schwab, American Industrialist (1862-1939).
33. James M. Kouzes and Barry Z. Posner, *The Leadership Challenge.* (San Francisco: Jossey-Bass, 2003).
34. David Kirsch, Department of Cognitive Science, University of California, San Diego.
35. The article is a prelude to Dr. Gardner's *The Five Minds of the Future.* (Boston: Harvard Business Review Press, 2006).
36. Tojo Thatchenkery and Carol Metzker, *Appreciative Intelligence: Seeing the Mighty Oak in the Acorn.* (San Francisco: Berrett-Koehler Publishers, 2006).
37. Adele B. Lynn, *In Search of Honor-Lessons from Workers on How to Build Trust.* (Belle Vernon: Bajonhouse Publishing, 1998).
38. Todd Benjamin, "Arun Sarin, Encouraging Others to Shine," CNN World Business, 10 June, 2005.

39. "Pygmalion in Management," *Harvard Business Review OnPoint Enhanced Edition*, 01 September, 2002.

40. See also Jean-François Manzoni and Jean-Louis Barsoux, *The Set Up to Fail Syndrome*. (Boston: Harvard Business School Press, 1998).

41. For a description of the Galatea Effect and advice on how to use it to enhance employee performance, see Tom Massey's *Ten Commitments for Building High Performance Teams*. (Bandon, OR: Robert D. Reed Publishers, 2005).

42. See also Albert Bandura, *Self-Efficacy: The Exercise of Control*. (New York: Worth Publishers, 1997).

43. Interview of Carol Metzker on book she co-authored with Tojo Thatchenkery, *Appreciative Intelligence: Seeing the Mighty Oak in the Acorn*. (San Francisco: Berrett-Koehler Publishers, 2006).

44. James O'Toole, *Creating the Good Life-Applying Aristotle's Wisdom to Find Meaning and Happiness*. (New York and Emmaus: Rodale Inc., 2005).

45. Tom Rath and Donald O. Clifton, *How Full is Your Bucket: Positive Strategies for Work and Life*. (New York: Gallup Press, 2004). Also see the resources on the book's website, http://www.bucketbook.com.

About the Author

Bruna Martinuzzi is the President of Clarion Enterprises Ltd., a company which specializes in leadership, emotional intelligence, and presentation skills training. She is a facilitator, coach, author, and keynote speaker with over 25 years of leadership experience in the petroleum and technology industries. Bruna speaks six languages and holds a Bachelor of Arts and a Master of Arts degree from the University of British Columbia. She is the recipient of several awards, including the Izaak Killam Pre-Doctoral Fellowship, the Social Science and Humanities Research Council of Canada Award, and the BC Workplace Excellence Award for Unusual Innovation. She is the co-author of *The Power to Lead: Lessons in Creating Your Unique Masterpiece.* She lives in North Vancouver, British Columbia, Canada. For additional information on Clarion Enterprises Ltd. go to websites http://www.increaseyoureq.com or http://www.clarionenterprises.com. Bruna can be reached at bmartinuzzi@increaseyoureq.com.